Learn to Read Ancient Sumerian

Learn to Read Ancient Sumerian
An Introduction for Complete Beginners

Joshua Bowen
Megan Lewis

Digital Hammurabi Press
Mechanicsville, MD.

Library of Congress Control Number: 2019920293
ISBN: 978-1-7343-5860-5

Contents

Why a Sumerian Grammar?

When we founded our YouTube channel, *Digital Hammurabi* in 2018, we wanted to make Ancient Mesopotamia come alive to people of all walks of life. As Assyriologists (people who study the languages and culture of ancient Iraq), much of our training is in two very important languages from the Ancient Near East: Akkadian and Sumerian. As Josh specialized in Sumerian in his PhD program, we thought that it would be a good idea to make a series of videos teaching people to learn to read the Sumerian language. Of course, we assumed that there would be little interest in the topic; I mean, who would want to learn to read Sumerian, other than a small handful of people that like living in the basement of a library? Boy, were we ever wrong!

From the moment that we published the *Learn to Read Ancient Sumerian* video course on YouTube, it has consistently been the most viewed series on the Digital Hammurabi channel. Every week someone new asks for a Sumerian grammar that they can use in conjunction with the video series. There are many excellent and scholarly Sumerian grammars that brilliant Assyriologists have written, including books by Attinger, Thomsen, Edzard, Jagersma, Zólyomi, Foxvog, and Hayes;[1] however, there is no good introductory grammar to recommend for absolute beginners, particularly those who are working on their own. To date, the brilliant scholars who have written monumental Sumerian grammars have written them for people that already know Sumerian. These are the reference grammars that you use when you are translating through *Gilgamesh, Enkidu, and the Netherworld* or *Inanna's Descent to the Netherworld*, and you come across an unfamiliar Sumerian grammatical form. You already know the Sumerian language, and you can translate through these difficult compositions; but there are always things that are challenging to understand. In these moments, you turn to a reference grammar like some of the ones cited above in order to figure out the answer to that unclear grammatical form.

Unfortunately, if you don't already know Sumerian, and you want to pick up a book, read through it, and learn the language on your own, you are out of luck. That is, *until now.* The goal of this book is to teach you to learn to read Sumerian on your own (or in a classroom), even if you have had no experience or training in the language. This

---

[1] Full references to these publications can be found in the Bibliography.

Sumerian grammar is truly intended for the lay person. Although this is a book about Sumerian linguistics, there is only as much complex and "scholarly" language as necessary. When uncommon terms are used, like "comitative" or "agent", we've made every effort to explain exactly what that word means as it appears. There is also a glossary of grammatical terms at the end of the book so you can look up definitions if you need to! So, if you have always wanted to learn to read Sumerian, but you don't have the time or the money to attend a university, then this is the book for you!

The chapters are organized in such a way that you will learn the basics of the language in small, manageable pieces. This book can also be used in conjunction with our *Learn to Read Ancient Sumerian* video series on YouTube, allowing you, the student, to hear the lessons explained in video format.[2] Once book one is mastered, the student can move on to book two, which provides intermediate-level details on the Sumerian language. Rather than explaining every detail of a particular topic (the verb, for example), this book (the first in a three-part series on learning to read Sumerian) provides the basic information necessary to understanding the verb. More detailed information will be given in book two, and finally, in

---

[2] This book contains expanded and updated exercises, so they will not match the videos exactly. The bulk of the lessons are, however, the same.

book three of the series,[3] we will look at the advanced aspects
of the language. However, the majority of the basic concepts
necessary to read and understand the Sumerian language
will be presented in book one.

Before we begin our grand adventure into learning to read
Sumerian, a caveat should be stated. To the brilliant
Assyriologist reading this grammar - this book is in no way
intended to cover every detail of Sumerian linguistics. It is
not intended to be a reference grammar, and should not be
treated as such. Its purpose is to provide the interested
student a way to access Sumerian without the direct
instruction of a professor of the language. It is our hope that,
with a resource like this, we will see a new wave of excited
students, beating down the doors of our institutions, wanting
to become experts in the field of Assyriology.

With all of this in mind, it's time to begin your journey and
learn to read the world's first written language, Sumerian...
so come along for the ride!

---

[3] Books two and three forthcoming.

Thanks and Acknowledgements

First and foremost, our heartfelt thanks to Dr. Paul Delnero who gave both of us a (painfully) rigorous grounding in the Sumerian language. It is truly no exaggeration to say that this book would not have been written without him. Josh would also like to thank Dr. Konrad Volk for his generous mentoring and support during his Fulbright year in Tübingen, Germany.

We cannot possibly acknowledge every Sumerologist whose work on Sumerian grammar has contributed to modern scholarship's understanding of the language, but we thank them wholeheartedly. We are proud and humbled to stand on the shoulders of such giants.

Thank you to the friends and colleagues who generously gave their time to read the manuscript of this book. Your corrections helped immeasurably. Errors contained within these pages remain our own!

Finally, thank you to everyone who emailed, or left comments, suggestions, and questions on our YouTube channel, and Paul, who volunteered to produce additional learning resources to accompany the video series. You all confirmed that Sumerian is worth teaching outside of universities, and your feedback prompted the creation of this book.

Introduction

While some other ancient languages are relatively well-known (Greek, Latin, or even Biblical Hebrew), comparatively few people know (or are even aware of) Sumerian – the world's first written language. Appearing mostly on small tablets made of clay, written with curious 'wedge-shaped' signs, Sumerian writing was in use (and has been preserved from) over five thousand years ago!

Sumerian was spoken and written in a geographical region known today as "Mesopotamia", which corresponds roughly to modern-day Iraq. Sumerian was used primarily in southern Mesopotamia ("Sumer"), though cuneiform was used throughout all of Mesopotamia, as well as parts of Turkey, Syria, Iran, and the Levant. There were even letters written in cuneiform discovered in Egypt!

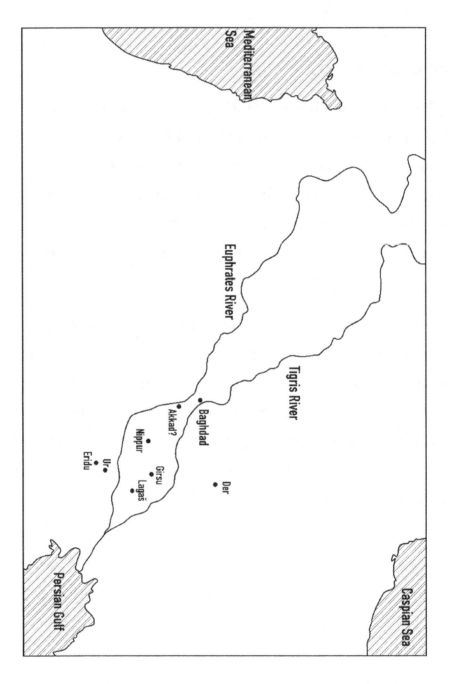

Map showing Mesopotamia, and the ancient cities mentioned in this book. The modern city of Baghdad is shown for context.

Sumerian was one of the most important languages in Ancient Mesopotamia. The Sumerian texts refer to their language as "Emekiengi" (/eme ki.en.gi/ "the language of Sumer"), as well as "Emegir" (/eme.gir₁₅/ "native language"). A dialect of Sumerian that was used by a specialized group of religious personnel was called "Emesal" (/eme.sal/ "thin/fine tongue"). There is no known language that is like Sumerian; scholars refer to it today as a "language isolate". While many suggestions have been made concerning languages that could be in Sumerian's linguistic "family", no suggestion has been shown to be valid to date. However, there was another influential language in the region that interacted with it: Akkadian. Both languages utilized the same cuneiform writing system, and had significant influences on each other.

The earliest Sumerian documents were less glamorous and romantic than we might hope, and mainly recorded administrative transactions. Over the more than 3,000 years in which the language was used, many different types of texts were composed, including administrative, literary, legal, and liturgical texts, not to mention incantations, letters, sign lists, and royal inscriptions! While there are a number of literary compositions that were written in the third millennium, the vast majority were composed in the first part of the second millennium BCE (known as the Old

Babylonian Period). It is from this period that we have extensive evidence for scribal education in Mesopotamia, where students learned to read and write Sumerian by copying a wide variety of compositions, including a vast array of literary texts.

In spite of its versatility, Sumerian was not to last as a living language; it died sometime in the late third or early second millennium. Despite this, Sumerian continued to be used in scholarly and cultic circles (much like the modern use of Latin) following its death as a spoken language. In fact, Sumerian compositions were copied and utilized at least until the end of the first millennium BCE!

The cuneiform signs that were used to write Sumerian are a little tricky to learn. In each chapter of this book, we will introduce you to a handful of commonly used cuneiform signs for you to memorize and learn to recognize. Although you might want to jump right in and read everything in cuneiform, I have found that it is much easier to learn the vocabulary, grammar, and syntax of the language in transliteration first. After the basics are mastered, it will be much more manageable to read more complex cuneiform, as opposed to learning both the language and the full writing system simultaneously. There are also several additional exercises in the appendices in which you can utilize your new-found knowledge of cuneiform signs, including a selection of Mesopotamian royal inscriptions.

Writing Sumerian in English characters (we refer to this as "transliteration") can seem a bit strange, and there are some common conventions that are used throughout this book (for example, /e$_2$ gal/ represents the signs /e$_2$/ and /gal/). However, unless you're already a trained Assyriologist, you're probably not going to be familiar with them, so here's a brief explanation to help! This book will often use forward slashes (/ /) to mark a syllable, word, phrase, or sentence as transliteration (for example, /lugal-e e$_2$ mu-un-du$_3$). If there are dashes (-) between syllables, this means that these are the actual signs that appear on the tablet; thus, if you see /e$_2$ gal-la/, you would know that if you went and looked at the tablet then you would see the signs /e$_2$/, /gal/, and /la/. However, if we want to *normalize* the Sumerian signs (that is, writing the grammatical structure they represent), we will place periods (.) in between the signs (for example, /e$_2$ gal.a/, showing the /a/ as the marker of the adjective). Other nuances in the notation system will be discussed as they come up in the lessons.

It might also be useful to briefly discuss an important online resource. In this grammar you will see references to "ePSD". While this might sound like some kind of disease, it stands for the "Electronic Pennsylvania Sumerian Dictionary". This is an extraordinarily useful resource, which not only provides definitions of Sumerian words, but lists of all possible meanings attributed to a particular cuneiform sign, as well as images of the signs themselves. It also allows you to search for the word you are looking up in the online database of Sumerian literary texts simply by clicking on the link. The ePSD website can be freely accessed online – simply search for "epsd Sumerian" using a web browser of your choice!

With all of this in mind, we can now begin our journey in Learning to Read Sumerian!

Chapter One

Cuneiform Signs and Sounds

Cuneiform Signs and Sounds

Learning to read any ancient language begins with learning the signs or symbols that the language uses to write its words and phrases. With languages like Hebrew, Greek, and Latin, the task is relatively simple, as they each use an *alphabet*: a fixed set of individual letters or symbols that represent the basic sounds of the language. Sumerian, on the other hand, uses a system of writing called cuneiform, which is used to write *words* and *syllables* rather than individual letters. That means there are MANY more signs to learn than what you will find in a standard alphabet. Thus, instead of initially learning all the many signs that are used to write the language (the cuneiform), we will learn to read the language primarily in English characters. However, with each lesson, the student will learn a handful of cuneiform signs, building a *repertoire* of sorts that will allow them to read simple cuneiform texts.

First, we must learn the basic sounds that appear in the Sumerian language, not only to know how the words generally sounded, but also to be able to interact with other people about the Sumerian language in a way that follows the general conventions of pronunciation.[4] These are the basic Sumerian sounds:

a	f<u>a</u>ther
b	<u>b</u>oy
d	<u>d</u>og
e	s<u>e</u>t, h<u>ey</u>
g	<u>g</u>irl
g̃	si<u>ng</u>er
ḫ	Lo<u>ch</u>
i	b<u>i</u>t, b<u>ee</u>
k	<u>k</u>ite
l	<u>l</u>ong
m	<u>m</u>an
n	<u>n</u>ice
p	<u>p</u>ark
r	<u>r</u>un
s	<u>s</u>wim
š	<u>sh</u>eet

---

[4] How Sumerian was pronounced is an extremely complicated issue, and this "pronunciation guide" is in no way intended to weigh in on the discussion. Our only goal here is to provide the student with a basic understanding of how we generally think the sounds were pronounced, and to give them the ability to interact with others who read and study Sumerian.

t	-	<u>t</u>ime
u		m<u>oo</u>, fl<u>oo</u>r
w		<u>w</u>ater
z		<u>z</u>ebra

As you can see, some of the sounds can vary, depending on the word in which the sound appears. Let's go through some of the letters with either foreign or varying sounds.

/e/

The sound /e/ can be either short (as in "s<u>e</u>t" or "b<u>e</u>t"), or it can be long (as in "h<u>ey</u>" or "w<u>ay</u>". In the Sumerian word eš, "shrine" (written with the cuneiform sign /eš$_3$/), the /e/ is short. The same is true for the grammatical marker -še, "to, toward" (written with the cuneiform sign /še$_3$/). However, the word e, "house" (written with the cuneiform sign /e$_2$/), is commonly pronounced like the /ey/ in the word "hey".

/g̃/

The nasalized /g/ sound is one that can give students some trouble. It is, generally speaking, an /ng/ sound, as in "si<u>ng</u>er". Thus, the Sumerian word dig̃ir, "god", is actually pronounced "di<u>ng</u>ir". The word pirig̃, "lion", is pronounced "piring" with two short /i/ sounds. When the /g̃/ appears at the beginning of a word, such as g̃iš, "wood", it is pronounced "<u>ng</u>ish", although it tends to sound more like "<u>ny</u>ish".

/ḫ/

The sound that /ḫ/ makes is akin to the /ch/ in the German word *Loch*. It appears at the beginning of a word in the very common verbal prefix ḫe- (written with the cuneiform sign /ḫe₂/). The word ḫašḫur, "apple", contains an /ḫ/ in both the beginning and middle of a word, while ḫuluḫ "to be frightened" has the consonant at the beginning and the end of the word. In each case, it is pronounced /ch/.

/i/

The vowel /i/ can be pronounced short (as in "h<u>i</u>t" or "kn<u>i</u>t"), or it can be long (as the /ee/ in "b<u>ee</u>" or "kn<u>ee</u>"). Thus, the word nin, "lady", is pronounced with a short /i/. The /i/ in the divine name Enlil (written with the cuneiform signs /ᵈen-lil₂/[5]) is pronounced in the same way. However, the common word ki, "earth, land", is pronounced like the word "key", and the word ensi, "ruler", is pronounced with a long vowel sound "en-s<u>ee</u>".

/š/

The consonant /š/ sounds like the letters /sh/ in "<u>sh</u>ow" and "<u>sh</u>eet". The preposition mentioned above, -še, is pronounced

---

[5] The superscripted "d" in the name /ᵈen-lil₂/ is an Assyriological notation indicating the presence of the diĝir cuneiform sign, which can be used to indicate that the name following following it is divine. More on this later!

like the /she/ in the word "shed". The city named Lagaš ends in a /š/, and is pronounced "Lagash".

/u/

Finally, the vowel /u/ can be pronounced short (as in "floor"), or it can be long (as the /oo/ in "moo" or "boo"). Thus, the short /u/ in the word kur "mountain" is pronounced like the /oo/ in "floor", while the word lugal "king" is long, pronounced "loo-gal" (with the /oo/ in "moo").

What's with the Subscripted Numbers?

What do those little subscripted numbers mean next to letters (e.g., /me$_3$/, /du$_{11}$/, /du$_3$/, /i$_3$/, /g̃a$_2$/)? Well, as you can imagine, representing Sumerian chicken-scratch...I mean, cuneiform, in English characters, can be difficult. Those subscripted numbers are a tool used by Assyriologists to make the process a little easier. I mean, learning Sumerian is hard enough as it is, am I right?

There are many cuneiform signs that are *pronounced* in the same way: they are *homophonous*, as in the English words *dear* and *deer*, *be* and *bee*, and *hey* and *hay*. Thus, there are different signs that are pronounced *du*, but mean different things (e.g., /du$_{11}$/ "to say, speak"; /du$_3$/ "to build"; /du$_{10}$/ "to be good"). Each one is pronounced the same way, but they represent different cuneiform signs, and mean different things. Thus, in order to distinguish them when we write them in English, we put subscripted numbers next to them.

How Do Cuneiform Signs Work?

One of the most difficult aspects of learning Sumerian is mastering the cuneiform writing system. Cuneiform, or 'wedge-shaped' writing, was used to write both Sumerian and Akkadian, and could employ the use of several hundred signs in a particular period. While this may seem daunting at first, much of the fear and trepidation can be taken away if you realize that mastery of a basic set of signs will allow you to understand many Sumerian texts. In addition, with the resources available to us today (e.g., sign lists, online dictionaries, searchable databases), simply understanding how cuneiform signs "work" will go a long way. With that in mind, let's take a look at the three basic ways that cuneiform signs can be used in Sumerian.

Single Words

/e$_2$/ means "house" or "temple", the sign /a/ represents "water", and the sign /gu$_4$/ means "ox". The individual sign was impressed onto the tablet to indicate that particular word. Below is a list of cuneiform signs, the words that they correspond to, and their English translations:

e₂	house, temple	
lugal	king	
nin	lady	
tur	small	
dumu	son[6]	
nita	male, man	
munus	woman	
ama	mother	
me₃	battle	
kala	mighty, strong	
kur	mountain	
diĝir	god	

---

[6] A single cuneiform sign can have multiple meanings – the /tur/ sign can also be read as /dumu/!

Syllables

There is only so far that a language can go, however, if you can only represent individual objects or ideas. Cuneiform signs developed to accommodate a broader range of writing by having the signs also represent *syllables*. As the individual signs represented particular words, those signs began to be used to represent *sounds*, not the individual words. For example, the sign 𒈠 /ga/ means "milk", the sign ✳ /an/ means "sky, heaven", and ▷ /du₃/ represents the verb "to build". All of these signs can *also* represent phonetic values of those words, so the verbal form *gandu* (written /ga-an-du₃/ in cuneiform signs) does not mean "milk sky build", but instead "Let me build". Instead of creating a particular cuneiform sign to represent the verbal form *gandu*, they used the signs /ga/ and /an/ as *syllables* before the verb /du₃/ "to build".

In other words, in the verbal form /ga-an-du₃/, /ga/ and /an/ are being used as syllables to represent the sound /gan-/ in the verb *gandu*. With this principle of using word signs (or logograms) to represent phonetic values (e.g., /ga/ "milk" and /an/ "sky" to write /ga-an-/), the Sumerian language was able to represent a whole host of grammatical and syntactical forms, verbs declension, case markers... you name it.

To briefly recap, in Sumerian, a cuneiform sign can represent:

1. A word:  /e_2/ "house"
2. A syllable: 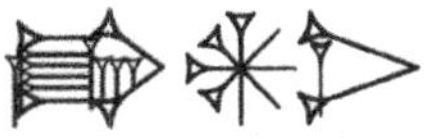 /ga-an-du_3/, used to write the verb *gandu*, not to mean "milk-sky-build".

There is one final way in which a cuneiform sign can appear: as a determinative.

Determinatives

If you hadn't noticed, Sumerian signs can be a little… confusing, and not just for us reading them today. There were times that people writing Sumerian wanted to make sure that, when they wrote a word, it would not be confused with something else. For example, the word guza /gu-za/ means "chair". If the writer wanted to let the reader know that the chair was made out of wood, they would write the sign  /g̃iš/ ("wood") before it (), which we write in English /$^{\text{g̃iš}}$gu-za/. The sign /g̃iš/ was not pronounced; it was simply written to let you know that the chair was made out of wood. The same was true for the names of gods. The name *Enlil* was given to one of the chief gods of the pantheon. When you wrote his name, you would not simply write /en-

lil₂/; you would put the sign ✳/diĝir/ ("god") before it: (✳ ◁
▦).

Notice that the words for "wood" and "god" are neither
pronounced nor translated; they are simply identifying the
following word as belonging to a particular category (wood or
deity). A sign that is used in this way is called a
"determinative"; it "determines" what kind of word the noun
will be. Signs that are used as determinatives can be written
before or after the word that they are attached to. Below is a
list of the most common determinatives, their meanings, and
whether they occur before or after the noun they relate to:

1. ĝiš   ĝišgu-za   made of wood

before noun

2. diĝir   ᵈen-lil₂   divine being

before noun

3. ki   eriduki   place name

after noun

4. ku₆   suḫurku₆   fish

after noun

5. mušen  tu-gur₄^{mušen} bird

after noun

Notice that, when we write the determinative in English characters, we superscript the word (or the letter, in the case of /ᵈ/ for /diĝir/), in order to indicate that the sign is being used as a determinative. When you see a superscripted form like this, it will most often indicate a determinative... and they appear a lot!

To sum up, if you see a Sumerian cuneiform sign, it will almost always be functioning in one of three ways:

1. A word:

      /e₂/   "house"

2. A syllable:

   /ga-an-du₃/   "*gandu*", not

"milk-sky-

build"

3. A determinative:

   ᵈen-lil₂   "Enlil"

Sumerian Nouns

We all remember from grade school that a noun is a "person, place, or thing". The same is true in Sumerian (whew!). Nouns are the basic building blocks of the language, and understanding how they are represented in a sentence is a critical part of learning to read Sumerian.

Many languages distinguish between masculine and feminine nouns. For example, in Spanish, *el chico* "boy" is masculine, while *la chica* "girl" is feminine. Sumerian has no such distinction. Instead, Sumerian distinguishes between *animate* and *inanimate*: humans (animate) vs. animals and objects (inanimate). This is visible, for example, in the possessive suffixes used by Sumerian. Instead of a male/female distinction, Sumerian uses the ending -ani to mean "his" or "hers", and the ending -bi to mean "its". Thus, the language distinguishes between animate and inanimate, or person and non-person.

There are two types of nouns that will appear in Sumerian: "single-sign nouns", and "compound nouns". Single-sign nouns are just what they sound like: a single cuneiform sign is used to represent a word; we have seen many of these in this lesson. For example, 𒂍 /e₂/ "house, temple", and 𒈗 /lugal/ "king". Compound nouns are formed with two or more signs that usually have independent meanings.[7] For example, the word /dub/ means "tablet"[8] and the word /sar/ means "to write". However, when you put them together, a /dub.sar/ is a "tablet-writer", or a "scribe". The word /e$_2$/ means "house", and when it is combined with the sign /gal/ "great", it means "palace" ("great house").

Plurals

Now that we know how nouns are formed, we can look at how Sumerian makes these nouns plural. In English, we usually put an /s/ on the end of a word to make it a plural (not always, obviously). Sumerian also has an ending that it attaches to the noun in order to make it plural; that ending is -ene (written /e-ne/). So, if /lu$_2$/ means "man", then /lu$_2$.ene/ would mean "men".

It would be nice if this ending were simply attached to all of the nouns that we see, wouldn't it? Alas, it can never be so simple. When we think about how English plurals are formed, we can't simply put an /s/ on every word either; sometimes we have to put /es/ instead. For example, the

---

[7] This is distinct from two or more signs that are strung together with a reading that is different from the individual signs (called a DIRI compound by Assyriologists). A good example is the writing of the name of the city Lagaš (ŠIR.BUR.LA^{ki}). DIRI compounds will be covered in book two of this series.

[8] The kind that you write cuneiform on!

singular form "car" goes to "cars" in the plural, but the singluar "box" is not written "boxs" in the plural; it is written "boxes". A similar type of variation occurs in Sumerian as well.

As the ending -ene starts with a vowel sound, it is often not simply attached to the noun. Thus, you will rarely find "gods" written /diĝir-e-ne/; it will usually appear /diĝir-<u>re</u>-ne/. The /r/ that is attached to the first /e/ of /-ene/ represents the consonant found at the end of the noun.

Repeating the /r/ in the first syllable of the ending /.ene/ makes pronouncing the ending easier. We refer to the final consonant of a word (or syllable) as an "auslaut" (from the German word *Auslaut* "final position"). So, we would say that the word /diĝir/ has an /r/ auslaut.

There are other ways in which Sumerian can make a word a plural. A rather intuitive way was simply to repeat the noun; if /lugal/ means "king", then /lugal-lugal/ meant "kings" or "all the kings". They would also make a noun plural by reduplicating the adjective (we will learn about adjectives shortly). The word /lugal/ means "king", and /gal/ is the adjective "great". If you write /lugal gal/, it means "great king" (the adjective comes *after* the noun). If they write the adjective twice (/lugal gal-gal/), it means "great <u>kings</u>".

Finally (and unfortunately), there are many instances in which a word written by itself can be either singular or plural. For example, if the word /lugal/ "king" appears in a sentence, it could either mean "king" or "kings", depending on the context.

Adjectives

Adjectives are words that describe something about the noun that they go with (or modify). When we say "the big dog" in English, "big" is an adjective that modifies "dog". What kind of dog? A *big* dog. The same is true in Sumerian. In English, the adjective comes *before* the noun, but in Sumerian, it comes *after* the noun. So, if /lugal/ means "king", and /gal/ means "great", then /lugal gal/ means "great king".

There are certain clues that can tell you that you are looking at an adjective in a Sumerian sentence. Our first clue is word order; if a word comes after a noun, we should look to see if it is an adjective. Another clue is that many (not all) adjectives have an /-a/ attached to the end of them. If we wanted to say "good woman", we would write /munus sag₉-ga/.[9] Notice that the final /g/ of the adjective /sag₉/ (the auslaut), is duplicated

---

[9] /munus/ "woman"; /sag₉/ "good"

in the following syllable, and is used to "attach" the /-a/ that is used to mark /sag₉/ as an adjective.

Another common example is the adjective /kala(g)/ "mighty, strong". Notice that there is a final /g/ that is written in parentheses at the end of the word /kala/. This means that the word /kala/ has a /g/ auslaut, but the /g/ is not always written in cuneiform. Often, these types of auslauts will only appear when an ending is attached to the word (like the /-a/ used to mark the adjective). So, if we see /lugal kala-ga/, and we know that /lugal/ means "king" and /kala(g)/ means "strong", then the /-ga/ must represent the /g/ from /kala(g)/, while the /a/ is the adjective marker.

It is very important to remember the word order in Sumerian, as there are a number of adjectives that often do not appear with an /-a/ adjective marker. For example, /lugal gal/ means "great king", even though it does not have the /-a/ adjective marker. The key is to remember:

1. Adjectives come after the noun they modify

2. They will sometimes have an /-a/ attached to them (usually with the auslaut consonant)

3. They may be unmarked (no /-a/).

Vocabulary

ama	mother
diĝir	god
dub-sar	scribe
dumu	son
e₂	house, temple
gal	big, great
ḫur-saĝ	mountain
kala(g)	mighty
kur	mountain
lugal	king
maḫ	magnificent
me₃	battle, combat
nin	lady
nita₂	man, male
tur	small, young
ur-saĝ	hero

Cuneiform Signs

an, diĝir

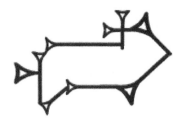

maḫ

gal

dumu, tur

e₂

kur

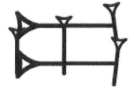

kala(g)

lugal

la

re

bi$_2$, de$_3$, ne

ki

Exercises

Normalize and translate the following sentences. Answers and explanations for all exercises in the book can be found in Appendix B – no peeking!

1. e_2

2. lugal

3. lugal maḫ

4. nin

5. dub-sar

6. dub-sar-re-ne

7. kur

8. lugal gal-gal

9. $nita_2$ kala-ga

10. me_3 gal-gal-la

11. ḫur-saĝ

12. kur gal-la

13. e_2 maḫ

14. kur-kur

15. dumu-e-ne

16. dumu tur

17. diĝir

18. diĝir-re-ne

19. ur-saĝ kala-ga

20. ama gal

Transliterate[10] and translate the following cuneiform:

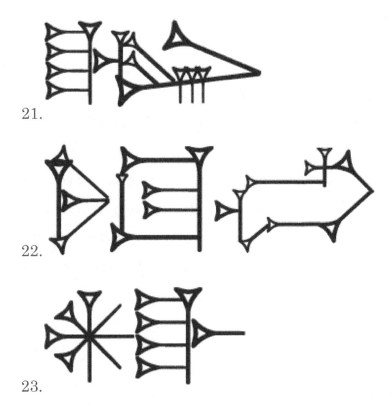

21.

22.

23.

Chapter Two

Introduction to Verbs and the Genitive

There are few things as frustrating as learning the verbal system of a foreign language. Past, present, and future tenses; passive and active; first, second, and third person... it can be enough to make you scream. Worry not! In *Learn to Read Ancient Sumerian*, we have strategically broken the verbal system up into manageable parts. In this lesson, we will provide a basic introduction to Sumerian verbs; in later lessons, we will look at the different tenses in Sumerian, how they modified verbs for person[11] and number[12], and the different parts of the "verbal chain".

In addition to a basic introduction to Sumerian verbs, we will investigate how to connect two nouns together using the word "of". For example, if we wanted to say "the house of the king" in Sumerian, we would say /e₂ lugal-la/; the /-a/ is the equivalent of the English word "of". This is called the

---

[11] Whether the subject of the verb is "I" (1st person), "you" (2nd person), or "he/she" (3rd person).

[12] Whether there is one or more person performing the action of the sentence.

"genitive". We will take a look at how to form the genitive in the second half of this lesson.

Take a deep breath, and let's venture into the world of Sumerian verbs...

Introduction to Sumerian Verbs

Before we start talking about "transitive" and "intransitive", or "passive" and "active" verbs in Sumerian, we should probably take some time to review these concepts in English grammar. Let's start with the difference between "transitive" and "intransitive" verbs. What is the difference between the following two sentences:

1. Johnny walks.

2. Johnny hit the ball.

Beside the actions themselves (walking and hitting), in the first sentence, Johnny is just performing an action (walking). However, in the second sentence, Johnny is doing something to something else (called the "direct object" in grammatical terms). So, in English, there are two types of verbs that we can use: verbs where the subject does something to something else, and verbs where it doesn't. If the subject (Johnny) is doing something to a direct object, we refer to the verb as being "transitive". You can think of it as the type of verb where the subject is "transferring" the effects of the verb to the direct object (Johnny is transferring the effects of "hitting" to the "ball"). If there is no direct object, we call the verb "intransitive".

Sumerian has the same distinction; the verb /e₃/ "to go out" does not have an object (you don't "go out" something), so it will be intransitive. In contrast, the verb /du₃/ "to build" needs an object (you build *something*), so it will be transitive. You can always tell if a verb is transitive or intransitive if you ask the question, "Is the subject doing something *to something else?*"[13]

Now that we understand "transitive" and "intransitive", let's take a quick look at "passive" vs. "active". When the subject of a transitive verb (Johnny in our sentence about hitting the ball) acts upon something else, that is an "active" verb. There are times, however, when the subject is actually *receiving* the action of the verb in the sentence. Take, for example, "Johnny was hit by the ball". Johnny is the subject, but he is no longer doing the hitting (I guess the ball got tired of being

---

[13] In our example above, "to walk" can be both transitive or intransitive in English. In the example given above, it is intransitive because the verb has no object. A transitive use of "to walk" would be 'Johnny walked the dog', as 'dog' is the object of the verb.

hit). This is a "passive" sentence, because the subject is receiving the action of the verb.

We also see active and passive verbs in Sumerian. For example, the verb /šum$_2$/ "to give" is usually active ("he gave the gift to the man"). However, as we will discuss shortly, Sumerian uses "participles", and these are often passive: /šum$_2$-ma/ "given" (passive). But more on this later.

Verbs and the Verbal "Chain"

Sumerian sentences look very different from those in English. The sentence "The king built the house" would be written in Sumerian as /lugal-e e$_2$ mu-un-du$_3$/, woodenly "king house he built". Without going into detail, I want you to see the basic structure of the verb, and its place in the sentence. So, let's take a look at this example sentence.

/lugal-e e$_2$ mu-un-du$_3$/

The word /lugal/ means "king", and the /-e/ attached to it indicates that /lugal/ is the subject of the verb, meaning that the king is the person performing the action (it is called the "ergative"). So we would translate /lugal-e/ "the king" (as the subject of the sentence). Of course, we know by now that /e$_2$/ means "house" or "temple", which leaves the form /mu-un-du$_3$/. This form is made up of two main parts: the "verbal base"(the part that carries the primary meaning of the verb, in this case, /du₃/ meaning "to build"), and the prefixes that come before (and sometimes after) the "verbal base" (in this case, /mu-un-/).

Now, we know that /lugal/ "king" is the subject of the sentence because of the /-e/ (the "ergative" marker) that is attached to it, but there is another clue that helps us figure that out: word order. Generally speaking, the word order in a Sumerian sentence is SUBJECT-OBJECT-VERB (SOV), which is what we see here. The word /lugal/ is the subject, /e₂/ is the object, and /mu-un-du₃/ is the verb, which is made up of the "verbal base" and the prefixes that come before it. This is how a great majority of Sumerian sentences will be constructed.

Now that we understand the basic structure of a Sumerian sentence, and how a Sumerian verb will appear, let's take a look at some of the fundamental facts about verbs. First, there are two basic types of verbs that are used: "simple" and "compound" (sounds a lot like the nouns, huh?). Simple verbs are just the verbs themselves (accompanied by the requisite verbal prefixes): /du₃/ "to build", /e₃/ "to go out", /gi₄/ "to return", /dim₂/ "to form, fashion", /e₁₁/ "to ascend/descend", and so on. In the example sentence above, the verbal form /mu-un-du₃/ is a simple verb.

In addition to a "simple" verb, there is a "compound" verb. These verbs not only contain a verbal base, but they also have a noun that is closely associated with the verb. Examples of this in English might be "fly-fishing" or "horseback-riding", where the verbs "fishing" and "riding" are so closely linked with the noun that the two are essentially inseparable. An example of a compound noun in Sumerian is /inim—gi₄/. The word /inim/ means "word", and /gi₄/ means "to return", so the verb literally means "to return a word", or "to answer, reply".

Other examples of compound verbs include /gu₃—de₂/ "to speak" (literally "to pour out the voice") and /igi—ĝar/ "to look at" (literally "to set the eye"). When compound verbs are written in a sentence, it looks like this: /igi mu-un-ĝar/, where the noun (/igi/) comes before the verbal chain, which contains the verbal base. Finally, take note of the convention of writing a dash in between the noun and verbal base when writing a compound verb in its lexical form (how it would appear in a dictionary). Simple verbs are written with just the verb (/du₃/), while compound verbs are written with the noun and the verb separated by a hyphen (/inim—gi₄/). We will cover compound verbs in detail in a later lesson.

Participles

Participles are words that look like verbs, but are used like adjectives or nouns, as in "the <u>running</u> man" (adjective) or "<u>running</u> is fun" (noun).[14] In English, they usually appear with an /-ing/ ending (running, swimming, jumping). In Sumerian, participles function in a similar way, but instead of 8using an /-ing/ ending (as in English), Sumerian adds an /-a/ to a verbal base.

For example, if we wanted to say "the rising sun", we would write /^{d}utu e$_3$-a/, where /^{d}utu/ is the name of the sun god, Utu, and the verb /e$_3$/ means "to go out".[15] Notice two things about the verbal form /e$_3$-a/; first, there are no prefixes before it (e.g., /mu-un-.../), and second, there is an /-a/ attached to the end of the verb. As a rule of thumb, if an /-a/ is attached to a verb with no prefixes, try translating it as a participle. If the verb /šum$_2$/ means "to give", and you see the form /šum$_2$-ma/,[16] try translating it as a participle: either "giving" or "given" (passive).

---

[14] Technically, verbal nouns are called "gerunds" in English, although Sumerian does not make this distinction.

[15] The sun "going/coming out" is how they described the sun "rising".

[16] Remember, the /m/ in /-ma/ represents the auslaut of /šum$_2$/.

The Genitive ("of")

Everybody likes to own stuff, and telling people that something belongs to someone is an important part of our everyday lives. In English, we do this in several ways: we can use words like "my", "your", "his", which are called "possessive pronouns". We can also add an /'s/ to the end of a word to show ownership; if we want to say that the toy truck belongs to Johnny, we say, "the toy truck is Johnny's" or "that is Johnny's toy truck". However, if we are being more formal, we can use the word "of": "that is the toy truck of Johnny".

We are more familiar with this type of construction in writing. People may write about "the house of the king" rather than "the king's house", or "The Day of the Lord" rather than "The Lord's Day". In any case, Sumerian also has the ability to show possessive relationships between two nouns: it uses the ending /-ak/. For example, if we wanted to say "the house of the king", we would (in theory) write /e$_2$ lugal.ak/ (even though the /-ak/ comes after the second noun, you translate it first in English).

Unfortunately, the ending /-ak/ is never actually written this way. Sumerian doesn't like to end words with a final /k/, so our example sentence would actually be /e$_2$ lugal-la/, where the /l/ in the syllable /-la/ represents the auslaut, and the /a/ in /-la/ represents what is left of the genitive marker /-ak/.

Now, don't lose hope! The /k/ will show up if something comes after the /-ak/. For example, if we wanted to say "The sons of the king" (/dumu/ "son"), we would write /dumu lugal-la-ke₄-ne/. Let's break that form down a bit; we would "normalize" (or write out all of the grammatical parts of the sentence in an understandable way) like this:

/dumu lugal.ak.ene/

We recognize all of the parts of this construction, right? We know /dumu/ and /lugal/, and the /-ak/ is the genitive marker ("of"), and the /.ene/ is the plural marker.

You can see two things from this example. First, both of the letters /a/ and the /k/ of the genitive marker /-ak/ are written, since the ending /.ene/ comes after it. Second, you can see that the plural marker /.ene/ doesn't go with /lugal/, but with /dumu/. But why? Why wouldn't we translate this "the son of the kings"? It is because Sumerian thinks of two words that are connected by the genitive "of" to be, essentially, a single unit. In other words, Sumerian treats this form like this: /[dumu lugal.ak].ene/, which we can think of like this: [son of the king].plural. If they wanted to write "son of the kings", we would see /dumu lugal.ene.ak/. We will come back to this principle in later lessons.

So, we have seen that, unless something comes after the genitive form /-ak/, the /k/ won't be written. Interestingly enough, there are some instances when you won't see *any* part of the form /-ak/ at all! We noted that the Sumerians did not generally like to pronounce /k/ at the end of a word. Similarly, if a word ends in a vowel (leaving no auslaut to attach to the /a/ of /-ak/), they generally will not write the /a/! So, in the phrase "the lady of Girsu" (/nin/ "lady"), they would write /nin g̃ir₂-su/, which we would normalize /nin g̃ir₂.su.ak/.

There are, however, some instances in which the /a/ of /-ak/ *will* appear when the form ends in a vowel. For example, we saw earlier that the ending /-ani/ means "his/her" (/lugal.ani/ would mean "his/her king"). If we wanted to say "the house of her king", we would likely see the form /e₂ lugal-la-na/, which we would normalize /e₂ lugal.ani.ak/. Notice that the /a/ of /-ak/ "replaces" (contracts with) the /i/ of the ending /.ani/.

That was a lot of variation in the writing of the genitive; let's try to simplify it. Here are the general rules:

1. If the noun ends in a consonant: /-a/ only (usually attached to the auslaut).

2. If the noun ends in a vowel: not written, or replaces the vowel (in certain cases.)

3. If something follows the /-ak/: the /k/ will be written.

One final note on the genitive: there is a funny little construction where instead of writing "the house of the king", they will write "of the king, his house". How will it look in Sumerian? A little something like this: /lugal-la e₂-ni/. Okay, let's break that down. The /la/ on /lugal/ contains the /l/ from the final consonant of /lugal/, and the /a/ of the genitive /a(k)/. So, we would read that, "of the king..." The /e₂-ni/ represents /e₂.ani/ (notice there is no /a/, since /e₂/ ends in a vowel), and we would translate that, "his house". When we put them together we get: "of the king, his house". This construction is called the "anticipatory genitive". Since the word order is reversed, you don't get to see the first word until later... so you are anticipating it! Clever, huh?

Tips on Translating that Pesky /-a/

It's at this point that students say, "They use the ending /-a/ for EVERYTHING!" That's true, that's true. There are many grammatical forms that are written /-a/ (there are actually more to come). But there is nothing to fear! Sumerian usually gives you little clues that let you know which /-a/ they mean. Below are some tips on distinguishing between the three cases that we have learned in which the ending /-a/ will appear on a form: the adjective, participle, and genitive.

1. Is it an adjective? Try to translate it as an adjective.

2. Is it a verb? Try to translate it as a participle (try a passive translation of the verb)

3. Is it a noun?

   a. Is there another noun directly before it? Try to translate it as a genitive ("of").

   b. No noun directly before it? We will learn about the other possibilities in a later lesson.

Vocabulary

a—ru	to dedicate
bad$_3$	wall
du$_3$	to build
du$_{11}$	to say, speak
e$_3$	to go out
ensi$_2$	ruler
gu$_3$-de$_2$-a	Gudea
gub	to stand
g̃ar	to set, place
g̃en	to go
ki—ag̃$_2$	to love
ki-en-gi	Sumer
ki-uri	Akkad
nig̃$_2$	thing
šum$_2$	to give
uri$_5{}^{ki}$	Ur

Cuneiform Signs

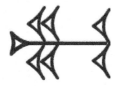

mu

a

ur

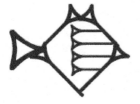

na

ni

du₃

me

en

Sumer (ki-en-gi)

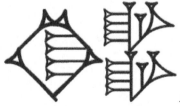

Akkad (ki-uri)

Exercises

Normalize and translate the following sentences:[17]

1. e₂ lugal-la

2. bad₃ gal

3. niĝ₂ šum₂-ma

4. diĝir-ra-ni

5. e₂ lugal-la mu-un-du₃

6. ki-aĝ₂-ĝa₂

7. ensi₂ ki-en-gi ki-uri-ke₄[18]

8. lugal-la e₂-ni

---

[17] Translate everything in the past tense until further notice!
[18] Ignore the /e/ attached to the /ke₄/.

Transliterate, normalize,[19] and translate the following cuneiform:

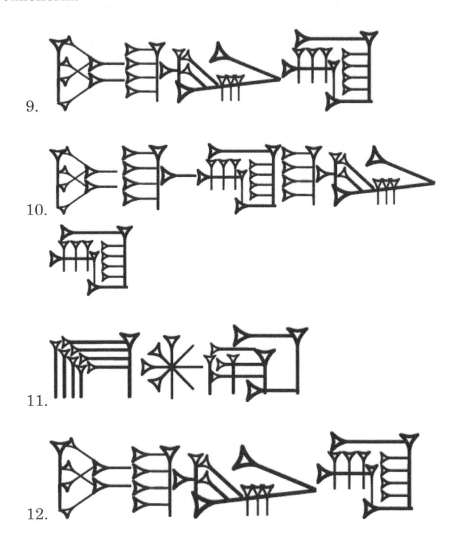

9.

10.

11.

12.

[19] Remember, normalizing is writing the grammatical structure represented by the signs.

46

13.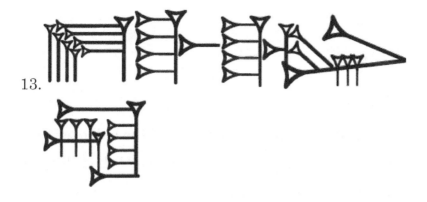

Chapter Three

Case Endings

When you read the sentence "Johnny hit the ball over the fence", how do you know who the subject is? What about the direct object? How can you tell where the direct object went? What if I interpreted this sentence: "The fence hit Johnny so hard that he went right over the ball!"? Crazy, right? And how do we know that I would be silly to interpret that English sentence in that way? Because English has "markers" that tell you how each word is functioning in the sentence.

For example, we know that "Johnny" is the subject of the sentence because it comes before the verb; we know that "the ball" is the direct object because it comes right after the verb. But what about "the fence?" Doesn't it come after the verb too? Yes, but it is "marked" by a separate word that tells you what role it plays in the sentence: "over". In other words, things like word order and prepositions tell us what the words and phrases in English sentences are doing.

But how do they do it in Sumerian? Well, we have already seen at least one of these markers that tell us how a noun is functioning in the sentence: the genitive /-ak/. We call this marker a "case marker" or a "case ending". Some of the most common case endings are prepositions.

We use prepositions all the time. "I'm going <u>to</u> the store", "this package came <u>from</u> the post office", "will you come <u>with</u> me <u>to</u> the game?" In English, prepositions are individual words that appear before the nouns that they govern (e.g., "<u>in</u> the house"). In Sumerian, however, prepositions are endings that are attached to nouns, just like the genitive case ending (/-ak/). In the same way as the genitive, you translate the preposition *before* the word it is attached to. For example, the ending /-še₃/ means "to" or "towards". The form /e₂-še₃/ (with /e₂/ meaning "house") would be translated "to the house".

Below is a list of the prepositions in Sumerian:

Sumerian	English	Grammatical term
/-ra/	to, for	dative
/-e/	at, near, up to	locative-terminative
/-ta/	from	ablative
/-še₃/	to, toward	terminative
/-da/	with	comitative
/-a/	in, into	locative
/-gin₇/	like, as	equative

We call these endings "case endings" because they are used to mark the "case" or "semantic category" that a noun belongs to in the sentence. And... what does that mean? Well, let's take the ending /-gin$_7$/ "like, as" (equative) as an example. If we were to write /lugal-gin$_7$/, we would translate that phrase "like a king". The ending /-gin$_7$/ is just a marker telling you that /lugal/ is in the "equative" case. Of course, you can see the word "equate" or "equal" in the word "equative", so if a word is in the "equative case", it simply means that the word it is attached to (e.g., /lugal/) is being "equated" with something else. Thus, we would say that /lugal/ is in the "equative case".

As we discussed above, languages indicate the cases (or semantic categories) of the nouns in their sentences in many different ways. In English, we write prepositions before the nouns to indicate their case (e.g., "like a king"). But in Sumerian, they attached case endings to the nouns in the sentence to tell you what roles the nouns were playing in the sentence. So, basically, when you see one of these case endings attached to a noun, think of it as an English preposition that is being attached to the end of the word, rather than coming right before it. Instead of writing "like a king", it would be as if we wrote "[a king]-like".

Now that we understand what case endings are, and how they are used, let's look at the basics of the individual case endings for prepositions.[20]

/-ra/ "to, for" (Dative)

The "dative" case ending /-ra/ is translated "to" or "for", and is only attached to humans or gods (things in the "animate" or "person" category). So, if you want to say, "he spoke <u>to</u> Enlil", you would write "he spoke Enlil-<u>ra</u>". It is also very common for something to be built or made "for" someone; /-ra/ is also used here. "He built the house <u>for</u> the king" would appear "he built the house the king-<u>ra</u>".

/-e/ "to, up to, near, at" (Locative-Terminative)

If the dative case ending /-ra/ is attached to animate beings (humans, gods), its counterpart for inanimate beings (animals, objects) is the ending /-e/, which we call the "locative-terminative". As one does not often talk to animals or objects, the locative-terminative (or "loc-term", as it is

---

[20] There are other nuances that these cases can have, but these will be explored in the intermediate grammar; let's keep things simple for now.

often called) is used in other ways that we will explore in a later lesson.

/-ta/ "from" (Ablative)

The "ablative" case ending /-ta/ is translated "from", and shows motion away from something or someone. Thus, if /uru/ means "city", then /uru-ta/ would be translated "from the city".

/-še₃/ "to, toward" (Terminative)

The "terminative" case ending /-še₃/ is the counterpart to the ablative /-ta/; it means "to" or "towards" (motion towards something). So, the phrase /uru-še₃/ would be translated "toward the city".

/-da/ "with" (Comitative)

The "comitative" case ending /-da/ is translated "with". The noun /da/ means "side", which makes sense; to be "with" or "at the side of" someone is the idea. Thus, /lugal-da/ would be translated "with the king".

/-a/ "in, into" (Locative)

The "locative" case ending /-a/ is translated "in" or "into". This is motion into something, or being "in" something. If someone walks "into" or is "in the house", it would appear /e$_2$-a/.

/-gin$_7$/ "like, as" (Equative)

As previously discussed, the equative case ending /-gin$_7$/ is translated "like" or "as" and compares two things. Thus, /lugal-gin$_7$/ would be translated "like a king".

Ergative

We now know how Sumerian tells the reader that certain nouns have prepositions associated with them, but how can we tell who the subject of a sentence is? Well, Sumerian marks the subject in two different ways, depending on the type of verb in the sentence. If the verb is intransitive (no direct object), there is no case ending or marker attached to the subject (we say that it is marked with a /-ø/ "zero")[21]. So, if /g̃en/ means "to walk", and we want to say "the king walks", we would write /lugal i$_3$-g̃en/,[22] and we would normalize it /lugal.ø i$_3$.g̃en/. In other words, the /-ø/ means that there is no special marker that is used to identify the subject of an intransitive verb.

---

[21] This is referred to as the "absolutive" case.
[22] /i$_3$-/ is the beginning of the verbal chain...ignore it for now!

However, Sumerian does have a special marker for the subject of a transitive verb (called the "agent" by Assyriologists); that case ending is written /-e/, and we call it the "ergative". When there is a sentence that has a transitive verb (one that has the subject doing something to a direct object), Sumerian will often put an /-e/ on the subject of the sentence. For example, if we wanted to write "the king built the house" (/du₃/ means "to build"), it would generally be written /lugal-e e₂ mu-un-du₃/. The /mu-un-/ is the first part of the verbal chain, which we can ignore for now, and /e₂/ "house" is the direct object, leaving /lugal-e/ as the "agent", or the subject of a transitive verb (in this case, /du₃/ "to build").

So remember:

o   Intransitive verb: /-ø/ (no case marker)

o   Transitive verb: /-e/ (ergative)

Copula

English uses the verb "to be" very frequently in sentences: "I <u>am</u> tired", "he <u>is</u> going to the store", "we <u>were</u> thinking of you". While Sumerian also has the verb "to be" that can appear as a normal verb, it often uses a standard ending that is attached to words or phrases. The most common endings

carry the meanings, "I am...", "you are...", and "he/she/it is..."
The forms are as follows:

Sumerian   English

/-me-en/   "I am"

/-me-en/   "You are" (singular)

/-am$_3$/   "He/she/it is"

There are plural forms as well, but we will stick with the
singular for the moment. These endings will often appear
attached to a noun (e.g., /lugal-me-en/ "I am the king"; /e$_2$-
am$_3$/ "it is the house". There are other nuances that are
associated with the copula that we will explore later.

Vocabulary

a	water
a-a	father
de$_2$	to pour out
e$_{11}$[23]	to ascend, descend
^{d}en-lil$_2$	Enlil
eš$_3$	shrine
g̃iš	wood
i$_7$[24]	river
igi	eye
igi—bar	to look at
il$_2$	to raise
munus	woman
ša$_3$	heart, middle
ŠIR.BUR.LA^{ki}	Lagaš
šu	hand
zi	true

---

[23] This verb can also be written /ed$_3$/.
[24] This noun can also be written /id$_2$/.

Cuneiform Signs

ĝiš

zi

šu

lil₂

ta

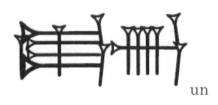

un

ma

ensi₂

lu₂

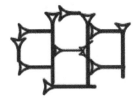

bad₃

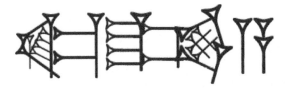

Gudea (gu₃-de₂-a)

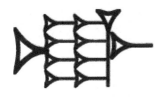

ak

Exercises

Normalize and translate the following sentences:

1. lu$_2$-da

2. e$_2$-še$_3$

3. a-e ba-diri[25]

4. lugal e$_2$-a i$_3$-g̃en[26]

5. lugal-le e$_2$ mu-du$_3$

6. ^{d}en-lil$_2$-ra ^{d}nanna bi$_2$-in-du$_{11}$[27]

7. uru-ta ^{d}utu i$_3$-g̃en

---

[25] Don't translate the /ba/ for now – this is a conjugation prefix and you haven't learned them yet! Just pretend it doesn't exist.

[26] Yup, /i$_3$/ is another conjugation prefix. Just translate the verb as a past tense.

[27] Yup, /bi$_2$/ is just like /i$_3$/ and /ba/ – ignore this one too! You can also ignore the /-in-/ in the verb as well.

Transliterate, normalize, and translate the following cuneiform:

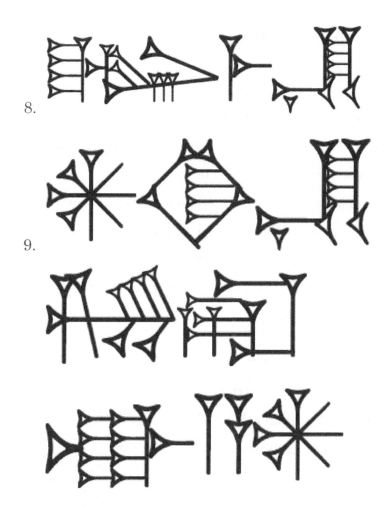

8.

9.

Chapter Four

The Verbal "Chain" Part One:

Case Elements

In Chapter Two, we learned about the basics of the Sumerian
verb: its parts and general structure, including the "verbal
chain" that often comes before the verb. In this chapter, we
are going to look at a major part of that verbal chain: case
markers. That's right! These are the case elements that
provide essentially the same information as the case endings
that we looked at in the last chapter. Only here, they are
written *in the verbal form.*

But why would they put the case elements in the verbal
chain if they are already on the nouns as case endings? They
are there to tell the reader, "look for a noun in this case in
the sentence!"[28] For example, the ablative case ending /-ta/
"from" can appear in the verbal chain as /-ta-/, telling you
that there is a noun in the ablative case somewhere in the
sentence. So, we might see a sentence that looks like this:
/lugal uru-<u>ta</u> mu-<u>ta</u>-g̃en/ "the king walked away from the
city" (/uru/ "city"). Here, the /-ta/ case ending "agrees" with

---

[28] There are other ways in which these case elements can function in the
verbal chain, but they will be taken up in the intermediate grammar.

the /-ta-/ case marker in the verbal chain. This type of "agreement" between case endings and verbal case elements is very common in Sumerian.

Before we move into the verbal case elements, I would like to take a second and provide a brief overview of the verbal chain. Please consider the following verbal form:

/nu-mu-ra-ab-g̃ar/

You probably recognize the verb /g̃ar/ "to put, place". But what about all of the stuff that comes *before* the verb? We learned in chapter two that the prefixes and suffixes that appear "around" the verbal base are part of what we call a "verbal chain". Sumerian does not use words like "will", "could", or "not" to form verbs like "will run", "could run", or "will not run". Instead of using separate words to adjust the meaning of the verbal base (like "will", "could", or "not"), it adds a variety of prefixes and suffixes to conjugate the verb.

If you look at the verb /nu-mu-ra-ab-g̃ar/ represented above, you can distinguish several different prefixes before the verbal base /g̃ar/ (like /nu-/, /-mu-/, /-ra-/, and /-b-/). Each of these prefixes has a particular function and appears in a preset order. For example, /nu-/ is basically the word "not;" it negates the verb. Thus, however we translate this verbal chain, it will basically have the meaning "not put, place" because of the negation /nu-/. The prefix /-mu-/ is a type of "conjugation prefix"; every verbal chain has one.[29] The /-b-/ tells you what is performing the action of the verb – more on this later.

As you can see, the verbal chain can contain a lot of information about the verb, including case elements. The /-ra-/ in this verbal form is the "dative" case element, 2nd person singular ("to/for you"). In the same way that the /-ta-/ in /mu-ta-g̃en/ told you to go and look for a /-ta/ case ending in the sentence, the /-ra-/ tells you that there is a "you" (singular) in the sentence somewhere that the subject is doing something "to" or "for".

Forms of the Verbal Case Elements

Now that we understand the basic principle of the verbal chain and the case elements that often appear in it, let's take a look at the way these case elements will look. We will begin with the dative.

---

[29] I bet you know what I'm going to say…don't worry about this right now. There will be more information on it later. Promise.

Dative "to/for"

Sumerian	Person	English
/ma-/	1st person singular	to me
/-ra-/	2nd person singular	to you
/-na-/	3rd person singular	to him/her
/-me-/	1st person plural	to us
???[30]	2nd person plural	to you
/-ne-/	3rd person plural	to them

We remember that the dative case ending on nouns is /-ra/, so /lugal-ra/ would be translated "to/for the king". If the writer wanted to "cross reference" the dative by writing it in the verbal chain, they would use one of the above forms. The 1st singular form is the odd one out.

Comitative "with"

There is only one form of the comitative in the verbal chain: /-da-/. Nice, huh? Sometimes, however, the writer wants to tell the reader "with *whom*". In other words, if the verb is /gub/ "to stand", and there is a /-da-/ in the verbal chain, we would say something like "stood with". But this leads us to ask, "with whom?". Sumerian has a way of telling us the "whom";

---

[30]Form unknown.

they sometimes add a letter directly before the form /-da-/ to act as a pronoun. Take a look at the following chart:

Sumerian	Person	English
/.ø.da/	1st person sg.	with me
/e.da/	2nd person sg.	with you
/n.da/	3rd animate sg.[31]	with him/her
/b.da/	3rd inanimate sg.	with it

As you can see, there is no special marker for the 1st singular (indicated by the "zero" /ø/). The 3rd singular endings will not appear in the writing system as just an /n/ or /b/; rather, they will be part of a syllable with a vowel (for example, /mu-un-da-gub/ or /mu-ub-da-gub/).

Locative "in"

The locative case element /-ni-/ deserves some attention. We remember that the locative on the noun is written with an /a/, so if we saw /e₂-a/, we would translate it "in(to) the house". Instead of using an /-a-/ in the verbal chain as the locative, Sumerian uses /-ni-/. Thus, in the sentence /e₂-a ba-ni-g̃en/,[32] we would identify the /-a/ on /e₂/ as the locative,

---

[31]Remember, Sumerian doesn't distinguish grammatically between male and female, but between animate (humans and deities) and inanimate (buildings, animals, plants and so on).
[32] Remember this /ba/? It's another conjugation prefix. Remember what to do with them? Right. Ignore it!

meaning "into the house". The verb /g̃en/ means "to go, walk". The /-ni-/ in the verbal chain would correspond to or "cross reference" the /-a/ on /e₂/.

It should be noted that the complete form /-ni-/ does not always appear in the verbal chain; there are many instances when only the /n/ of /ni/ is retained in the writing. So, if you see the form /ba-<u>an</u>-g̃en/, the /-an-/ could very well represent the locative /-ni-/.

Ablative "from" and Terminative "toward"

The remaining two verbal case elements are rather straightforward, and will thus be grouped together. The ablative "from" on the noun has the form /-ta/, and this is mirrored in the verbal chain (/-ta-/). The terminative "to, toward" appears as /-še₃/ on the noun, and a very similar form /-ši-/ appears in the verb.

Vocabulary

amar	calf
an-ub-da	corner
babbar	white
geme$_2$	female worker
g̃i$_6$-par$_4$	Gipar,[33] cloister
kalam	land
kar	quay
ku$_3$	pure, holy
ku$_4$	to enter
ku$_3$-babbar	silver
limmu$_2$	four
nam-til$_3$	life
^{d}nanna	Nanna
nibru^{ki}	Nippur
til$_3$	to live
u$_3$	and
u$_4$	day

---

[33] A specific building in the religious precinct.

Cuneiform Signs

a$_2$

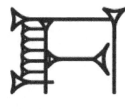

da

še$_3$

niĝ$_2$

si

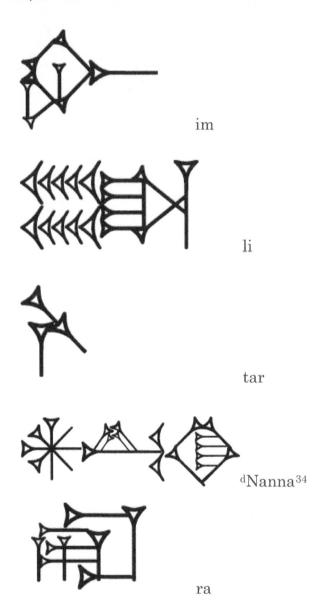

im

li

tar

^dNanna[34]

ra

---

[34] Do these individual signs look familiar? You have seen two of them before! When written together like this, the signs /^dšcš.ki/ represents the name of the moon god, Nanna.

Exercises

Normalize and translate the following sentences:

1. ^{d}en-lil$_2$-e ^{d}nin-g̃ir$_2$-su-še$_3$ igi mu-ši-bar[35]

2. lugal-ra ^{d}utu mu-na-du$_{11}$

3. lu$_2$-da mu-un-da-gub

4. kalam-ta dig̃ir mu-ta-g̃en

---

[35] igi-bar is a compound verb – now's a good time to test out your skills with ePSD! (Or you can look at the vocabulary appendix. We won't judge you).

Transliterate, normalize, and translate the following

cuneiform:[36]

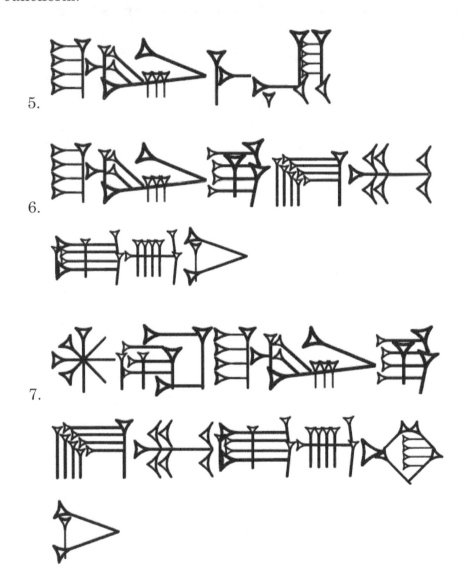

5.

6.

7.

---

[36] You haven't learned about all of the grammatical elements found in some of these examples, so don't worry if you're not sure what everything is doing. Just focus on the parts you do recognize!

Chapter Five

Verbal Inflection

What is "Inflection"?

We have looked briefly at some of the basics of Sumerian verbs, but we have not yet examined how they are changed in order to indicate *who* or *what* is doing the action of the verb. So, let's see how the verbs are "inflected". What does "inflection" mean? Inflection refers to the ways in which a word can change in order to alter its meaning. Let's take a look at some English examples:

The verb "jump"

Infinitive:	"<u>to</u> jump"
Present:	"jump<u>s</u>" or "<u>is</u> jump<u>ing</u>"
Past:	"jump<u>ed</u>"
Future:	"<u>will</u> jump"

The verb "sit"

Infinitive:	"<u>to</u> sit"
Present:	"sit<u>s</u>" or "<u>is</u> sitt<u>ing</u>"
Past:	"s<u>a</u>t"
Future:	"<u>will</u> sit"

Here we see several ways in which English modifies a verb in order to change the meaning. Words can be added before the verb ("<u>to</u> jump", "<u>will</u> jump"), or endings can be attached to the verb itself ("jump<u>ing</u>", "jump<u>s</u>"). In addition, English verbs will sometimes change the actual form of the verb in order to alter the meaning ("s<u>i</u>t" to "s<u>a</u>t;" "f<u>a</u>ll" to "f<u>e</u>ll;" "sw<u>i</u>m" to "sw<u>a</u>m"). Similarly, Sumerian will modify the form of the verb in order to change the meaning. There are prefixes, suffixes, and changes to the actual verbal base. We will explore some of these changes later in this lesson.

Tense in Sumerian

Tense can be a very important part of a language. Knowing that something happened in the past, present, or future makes all the difference in the meaning of a sentence. While the Sumerian verbal system is not the same as English, there are enough similarities to make useful comparisons. There are basically two "tenses" in Sumerian: past (called *ḫamtu*) and present/future (called *marû*).[37] Each tense has a specific way (or ways) that it modifies the verb. In this discussion, we will only give examples of verbs in the 3rd person singular, as

---

[37] It is, strictly speaking, not precise to speak about "tenses" in Sumerian; rather, we should focus on "aspect". However, this distinction is (in my opinion) unnecessary at this stage of learning. Thinking in terms of past and present/future "tense" will suffice for the time being.

it is extremely common. We will begin by discussing the past tense (*ḫamtu*) form of the verb.

The *ḫamtu* verb is considered to be the regular or basic form of the verb. When we say "regular" or "basic", we mean that the verbal base is generally not modified or reduplicated, which is common in the present/future tense (*marû*).[38] Here are some examples of *ḫamtu* verbs in the 3rd person singular:

Sumerian	English
/du$_3$/	to build
/mu-un-du$_3$/	he built
/la$_2$/	to extend; to hang
/mu-un-la$_2$/	he hung
/šum$_2$/	to give
/mu-un-šum$_2$/	he gave
/dim$_2$/	to form, fashion
/mu-un-dim$_2$/	he formed

You will immediately notice that the form of the verb that you see in the vocabulary lists or dictionaries (known as the "lexical" form) looks the same as the *ḫamtu* verbal base. In addition, in each of the examples, there is an /n/ that appears

[38] Reduplication is when a verbal base is written twice; for example: /mu-un-na$_8$-na$_8$/.

directly before the verbal base (e.g., /mu-u<u>n</u>-šum$_2$). Without going into any real detail (this will be saved for a later lesson), that /n/ marks the 3rd person subject of a transitive *ḫamtu* verb, "he/she". The important thing to remember here is that the *ḫamtu* (past tense) stem uses the regular or "lexical" form of the verb.

The *marû* (present/future) stem, however, will often modify the verbal base in such a way that it may not look the same as the lexical form. For example, the verb /g̃ar/ "to put, place" is written /g̃ar/ in the *ḫamtu* (as expected), but is written /g̃a$_2$-g̃a$_2$/ in the *marû*. The verb /du$_{11}$/ "to say, speak" is written /du$_{11}$/ in the *ḫamtu*, but /e/ in the *marû*. Of course, the *marû* verb does not always change the form of the verbal base; sometimes it simply adds a suffix. Let's take a look at the three ways in which a *marû* (present/future tense) verb can be formed.

Marû Form #1: Add an /-e/

Many Sumerian verbs do not bother modifying or reduplicating the verbal base in order to form the <u>*marû*</u> (present/future tense); they simply add an /-e/ to the end of the verb. Consider the following examples:

Sumerian	English
/la$_2$/	"to hang, extend"
/mu-la$_2$-e/	"he will hang"
/bad/	"to open"
/mu-bad-e/	"he will open"
/dim$_2$/	"to form, fashion"
/mu-dim$_2$-e/	"he will form"

As with the /n/ that appeared before the verbal base in the *ḫamtu* marking the subject, here we see an /-e/ attached to the verbal base in the *marû*. And as with the *ḫamtu* examples above, these are 3rd person singular *marû* verbs. We will learn the full paradigm[39] for both the *ḫamtu* and *marû* verbs in a later lesson.

So, you can form the *marû* by adding an /-e/ to the verbal base... but how else is it done?

Marû Form #2: Double the Verbal Base

Another way that the *marû* can be formed is by doubling the verbal base; we call this "reduplication". For example, the verb /gi$_4$/ "to turn, return" is written /gi$_4$-gi$_4$/ in the *marû*. The

---

[39] A paradigm is all of the ways a verb can be written to account for person and number.

verbal base /gi$_4$/ is simply doubled to form the present/future tense. Other examples include /gul/ "to destroy" (/gul-gul/ in the *marû*) and /kar$_2$/ "to shine" (/kar$_2$-kar$_2$/ in *marû*).

There are some verbs that, while they reduplicate, will also modify the verbal base when reduplicating. In an example above, we noted that the verb /g̃ar/ goes to /g̃a$_2$-g̃a$_2$/ in the *marû*. Thus, when /g̃ar/ reduplicated, it also dropped the final /r/ in both forms. A similar type of modification occurs with the verb /nag̃/ "to drink;" in the *marû* it changes to /na$_8$-na$_8$/, dropping the final /g̃/.

Okay, you can add an /-e/ and double ("reduplicate") the verbal base... anything else?

Marû Form #3: Change the Verbal Base

One final means of forming the *marû* is simply to change the shape of the verbal base. This is the same type of change that occurs in the English verbs *sit*, *fall*, and *swim*. You would not say "sitted", "falled", or "swimmed" to put these in the past tense; instead we say "sat", "fell", and "swam". Thus, instead of adding an ending to the verbal base, the base itself changes its form.

A good example of this is the common verb /du$_{11}$/ "to say, speak". In the *ḫamtu* singular, it is written /du$_{11}$/, but the *marû* singular is written /e/. Thus, instead of writing /mu-na-du$_{11}$/ (*ḫamtu*) "he said", you would write /mu-na-e/ (*marû*) "he will say". Another clear example of this type of change is the verb /de$_6$/ "to bring" (*ḫamtu*), which changes to /tum$_2$/ or /tum$_3$/ in the *marû*. There are *ḫamtu* and *marû* plural forms as well, but we will deal with these later.[40]

Ḫamtu Reduplication... Really?

We should note that there are instances when *ḫamtu* verbs will reduplicate, which often indicates plurality of some sort. We will deal with *ḫamtu* reduplication in Book Two, but generally speaking, if the verb is *intransitive*, then *ḫamtu* reduplication indicates a plural *subject*. However, if the verb is *transitive*, it indicates a plural *object*. In some cases, it is difficult to determine if the doubling represents a *ḫamtu* or a *marû* verb. One way of identifying which tense some verbs are in is to consider whether the reduplicated verb has changed its form. Remember /ĝar/ changing to /ĝa$_2$-ĝa$_2$/? That will only happen in the *marû*. Thus, if you see the form /ĝar-ĝar/, you can know that it is *ḫamtu* reduplication. The same is

---

[40] Appendix E contains some common irregular verbs that you may come across, and the different forms they take.

true of /nag̃-nag̃/; we know that this is *ḫamtu* reduplication, as the *marû* form would be /na$_8$-na$_8$/.

Vocabulary

ak	to do, make
alan	statue
bad	to open
de$_6$	to bring, carry
gi$_4$	to turn, return
gid$_2$	to be long
g̃eštug$_2$	ear, wisdom
igi—g̃ar	to look at
la$_2$	to extend, hang
ma$_2$	boat, ship
mu$_2$	to grow
na$_4$	stone
sag̃	head
sag̃—il$_2$	to raise the head
sag̃—gid$_2$	to become angry
temen	foundation
tud	to give birth
tug$_2$	clothing

Cuneiform Signs

nu

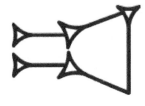

ab

ti

ri, re

gi

 nam

 gi₄

 bad

 e

Exercises

Normalize and translate the following sentences:

1. lugal-e e_2 mu-un-du_3

2. diĝir-re ĝeštug$_2$ mu-un-šum$_2$

3. lu$_2$-e alan mu-dim$_2$-e

4. nin uru-še$_3$ ba-gi$_4$

5. en e_2-še$_3$ ba-gi$_4$-gi$_4$

6. diĝir lugal-ra mu-na-du$_{11}$

7. nin diĝir-ra mu-na-e

8. ama-e a mu-tum$_2$

9. lugal-e niĝ$_2$ mu-de$_6$-de$_6$[41]

---

[41] Is this ḫamtu or marû?

Transliterate, normalize, and translate the following cuneiform:

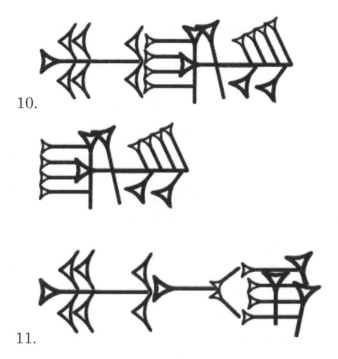

10.

11.

Chapter Six

Possession, Independent Pronouns, and Intransitive
Verbs

We are nearing the halfway mark in the book...
congratulations! Stay with it! You have a great deal of
Sumerian grammar already under your belt. In this chapter,
we will investigate more about possession, learn basic
independent pronouns, and see how to form the intransitive
verb.

Possession in Sumerian

"That's mine!" Like many parents, we hear the use of
possessive pronouns all the time. "My car", "your side", "her
fault"... you get the point. But of course, children are not the
only ones to use phrases of this sort. Possession and
ownership are extremely important aspects to any language.
In English, we use separate words and put them next to the
nouns that we own or possess. My, your, his, her, our, their,
etc.

Much to our surprise (just kidding), Sumerian uses endings
(suffixes) attached to nouns to show possession. For example,
the way you write "my" is with the ending /-$\tilde{g}u_{10}$/. So, if you

see /lugal-g̃u₁₀/, we would translate it "my king". Below are the singular possessive suffixes (we will deal with the plurals later):

Sumerian	English
/-g̃u₁₀/	my
/lugal-g̃u₁₀/	my king
/-zu/	your
/lugal-zu/	your king
/-ani/	his/her
/lugal.ani/[42]	his/her king
/-bi/	its
/lugal-bi/	its king

While these endings are relatively straightforward, there are a few things that we should briefly discuss. First, the 3rd singular ending /-ani/ is not written with one sign. In fact, as with the genitive /-ak/, sometimes the /a/ of /-ani/ will not appear in the writing. For example, when the noun ends in a vowel (e.g. in the form /lu₂-ni/ "his/her man"), the /a/ of /-ani/ "drops out", and the /ni/ is directly attached to the form /lu₂/. The same is true of /e₂/ "house", which would appear /e₂-ni/.

---

[42] This is usually written as /lugal-la-ni/ in cuneiform.

We should also remember that other grammatical markers can be added after these possessive endings. For example, if we were to write "the house of my king" in Sumerian, we would expect the grammatical construction to appear /e$_2$ lugal.g̃u$_{10}$.ak/. However, as we have seen, if words or forms end in vowels, and you attach a form beginning with another vowel, changes or deletions can occur. As we saw with the genitive, the /a/ of /-ak/ will often "swallow" and replace the preceding vowel. So, they would represent /e$_2$ lugal.g̃u$_{10}$.ak/ as /e$_2$ lugal-g̃a$_2$/. The final /k/ of the genitive /-ak/ drops off, as it appears at the end of the word (see Chapter Two), while the /a/ of the genitive replaces the /u/ of /-g̃u$_{10}$/, giving us the sign /-g̃a$_2$/ (/g̃u$_{10}$/+/a/). Similar changes will take place with the other possessive endings.

One final word should be said about possessive suffixes. As several markers can appear at the end of a noun (we just saw a possessive ending and the genitive together), it is good to know what order to expect them to appear in. If you remember the acronym PNC, you will always expect to see Possession, Number, Case, in that order. Let's look at an example so you can see for yourself!

In the form /lugal-zu-ne-ra/, we see several different endings (all of which you know, by the way) attached to the familiar noun /lugal/ "king". Going from left to right, we can recognize the following endings: /-zu/ "your", /.ene/ plural marker, and /-ra/ "to, for". Thus, it follows our expected pattern Possession (/-zu/), Number (/.ene/), Case (dative /-ra/). We would translate this phrase "to your kings" (/[{lugal.zu}.ene].ra/ = [{your king}.plural].to)

Independent Pronouns

"I like to run". "Susan saw him". "Jimmy spoke to her". We use pronouns all the time in English, and they can appear as the subject ("I like to run"), object ("Susan saw him"), or indirect object ("Jimmy spoke to her"). In Sumerian, they will sometimes use independent pronouns in a similar way. Below are the most common independent personal pronouns:

Sumerian	English
/g̃a$_2$-e/	I
/za-e/	you (singular)
/e-ne/	he/she
/e-ne-ne/	they

These forms can appear both as the subject and the object in a sentence. For example, you might see /e-ne e$_2$ mu-un-du$_3$/ "he built the house" (subject), but also /e-ne mu-un-de$_6$/ "he carried him" (object). Finally, case markers can be attached to these personal pronouns, so the form /e-ne-da/ would mean "with him", and /za-ra/ would be translated "to you".

Forming Intransitive Verbs

We have looked at basic aspects of the verb and some of the elements that can appear in the "verbal chain". We now turn to how intransitive verbs are formed. Remember, intransitive verbs are verbs in which the subject of the sentence performs the action of the verb, but no direct object is involved. For example, in the sentence "Timmy walks", *walks* is an intransitive verb. If you ask the question, "*What* is Timmy walking?" the answer is "nothing". If the subject of the sentence isn't *doing* the action *to* something (the direct object), then it is an intransitive verb. However, a transitive verb has the subject *doing something* to the direct object. "Sally kicked the football" contains a transitive verb. "*What* did Sally kick?" The ball.

Sumerian forms intransitive verbs differently than transitive verbs by adding endings to the verbal chain, whereas English treats them both the same way. The forms are listed below:

Sumerian	**Person**	**English**
/-en/	1st singular	I went
/i₃-g̃en-ne-en/		
/-en/	2nd singular	you went
/i₃-g̃en-ne-en/		

/-ø/   3rd singular   he/she went

/i₃-g̃en/

/-enden/   1st plural   we went

/i₃-re₇⁴³-en-de₃-en/

/-enzen/   2nd plural   you went

/i₃-re₇-en-ze₂-en/

/-eš/   3rd plural   they went

/i₃-re₇-eš/

---

[43] /re₇/ is the ḫamtu plural form of /g̃en/ "to walk, go".

Vocabulary

dab$_5$	to seize
dam	spouse
e$_2$-gal	palace
en$_3$—tar	to ask
^{giš}eren	cedar
gaba	chest
gaba—ri	to confront
gaba-šu-g̃ar	opponent, rival
g̃al$_2$	to be, exist; put
ḫal	to divide, distribute
ḫul	to destroy
ninnu	fifty
^{d}ninsun	Ninsun
šu—tag	to decorate, touch
tag	to touch
uru	city

Cuneiform Signs

ḫu

nun

tur₃

ma₂

ke₄

am$_3$[44]

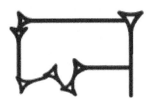

dim$_2$, gin$_7$

munus

zu

---

[44] These two should be familiar as well! Can you remember what the individual signs are called?

Exercises

Normalize and translate the following sentences:

1. e₂-g̃u₁₀; lugal-zu; ama-ni

2. bad₃-bi; nin-a-ni; lu₂-g̃u₁₀-ne-ra

3. g̃a₂-e e₂-a i₃-g̃en-ne-en

4. lugal-e za-ra mu-un-du₁₁

5. i₃-re₇[45]-en-de₃-en

6. e-ne-ne eden-ta i₃-re₇-eš

7. e-ne e₂-a i₃-ku₄

8. eden-ta uru-še₃ i₃-re₇-en-ze₂-en

9. lu₂ ᵍⁱˢeren-da uru-a i₃-g̃en

---

[45] Remember, /re₇/ is the *ḫamtu* plural of /g̃en/!

Transliterate, normalize, and translate the following cuneiform:

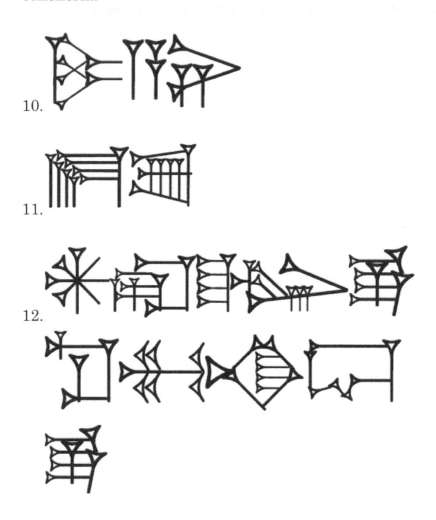

10.

11.

12.

13.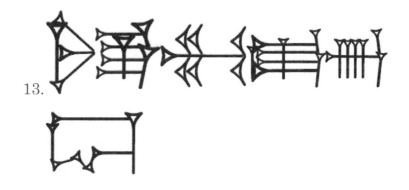

Chapter Seven

Transitive Verbs: Ḫamtu

In chapter six, we learned how Sumerian formed *intransitive* verbs – verbs without a direct object (like "Johnny runs", "Frank is swimming", and "Jill will walk"). There are many sentences, however, in which the subject of a sentence does something to something else in the sentence (for example, "Johnny hits the ball" or "Sarah flies the kite"). These are known as *transitive* verbs.

In English, the only thing that tells us who or what the subject and the object are in the sentence is word order. In Sumerian, the verbal form itself can tell you not only who the subject of a transitive verb is, but also who or what the object is. It does this by putting certain letters before and after the verbal base in the "verbal chain".

So, in the verbal form /mu-un-du₃/,[46] the /n/ that appears before the verbal base /du₃/ tells you that the subject

---

[46] Are you getting tired of this verb yet?

("agent") of the transitive verb /du₃/ "to build" is a "ḫamtu 3rd person singular animate" agent.[47]

In the chart below, we see the basic paradigm used to indicate or mark the agent of a ḫamtu transitive verb (we will learn the object markers in a later lesson):

Sumerian	Person
/-ø-/	1st Singular
/mu-gub/ /mu.ø.gub/	
/-e-/	2nd Singular
/mu-e-gub/	
/-n-/	3rd Singular Animate
/mu-un-gub/ /mu.n.gub/	
/-b-/	3rd Singular Inanimate
/mu-ub-gub/ /mu.b.gub/	
/-ø-VB-enden/	1st Plural
/mu-gub-be-en-de₃-en/ /mu.ø.gub.enden/	

---

[47] Ḫamtu, as we know, is the past tense in Sumerian. "3rd person singular" means "he/she" (rather than "they"), and "animate" means a person, rather than an animal or object.

/-e-VB-enzen/   2nd Plural

/mu-e-gub-be-en-ze$_2$-en/ /mu.e.gub.enzen/

/-n-VB-eš/   3rd Plural

/mu-un-gub-eš/ /mu.n.gub.eš/

Let's take a closer look at each of the *Ḫamtu* agent markers:

/-ø-/ 1st Singular

While this /ø/ "zero" symbol may still seem odd to you, the only thing that it indicates is that there was no special marker for the *ḫamtu* 1st person singular transitive verb.

/-e-/ 2nd Singular

When the 2nd person singular "you" is intended, an /e/ will appear before the verbal base.

/-n-/ 3rd Singular Animate

The 3rd person singular animate "he/she" is marked with an /n/ before the verbal base. This will usually appear attached to a vowel that appears in the previous syllable. For example, in the verbal form /mu-un-du$_3$/, the /n/ is the actual subject marker, but you could not simply write an /n/ in cuneiform. Thus, they would use a syllable that contained the vowel of the previous syllable (/un/ if preceded by /mu/, or /in/ if preceded by /bi₂/).

Notice that the /-n-/ is only used to indicate that a human (or god) is the subject of the transitive verb. If an animal (or an object) is the subject, they will use a /-b-/ (see below).

/-b-/ 3ʳᵈ Singular Inanimate

The 3ʳᵈ person singular inanimate "it" is marked with a /b/ before the verbal base. As with /n/, it will not be written alone, but will be attached to a vowel that generally mirrors the vowel of the previous syllable (/mu-ub-/, or /i₃-ib-/).

/-ø-VB-enden/ 1ˢᵗ Plural

Both of these "markers" (/ø/ and /enden/) should look familiar to you by now. As we have just seen, the 1ˢᵗ person singular is marked by a /ø/ before the verbal base, and we know from a previous lesson that the ending /enden/ is used for 1ˢᵗ person plural intransitive verbs. The 1ˢᵗ person plural ḫamtu simply combines these two forms in the verbal chain, putting one before and one after the verbal base.

/-e-VB-enzen/ 2nd Plural

As with the 1st plural forms, the 2nd plural markers are a combination of the 2nd singular /e/ and the intransitive ending /enzen/.

/-n-VB-eš/ 3rd Plural

Finally, the 3rd plural forms, as with the other plurals, have a form that comes before the verbal base (/n/) as well as an ending (/eš/). It follows the same pattern, mirroring the /n/ of the singular before the verbal base and using the same ending /eš/ as in the intransitive verbs.

Vocabulary

gu$_7$	to eat
i$_3$	oil
im	clay
inim	word
iti	month
ka	mouth
kaš	beer
naĝ	to drink
nam—tar	to decree a fate
ninda	bread
piriĝ	lion
še	grain
šu—zig$_3$	to raise the hand, to pray
tir	forest
tuš	to sit
zig$_3$	to rise; raise

Cuneiform Signs

mul

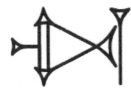

arad

bar

ru

ig

du

ib

ku, tuš

Exercises

Normalize and translate the sentences, and parse the verbs:[48]

1. lu$_2$-e e$_2$-a še mu-un-g̃ar

2. lugal-le-ne i$_3$ mu-un-de$_2$-eš

3. gu$_3$-de$_2$-a kaš bi$_2$-in-nag̃

4. pirig̃ eden-ta ba-ta-g̃en

5. pirig̃-e udu mu-ub-gu$_7$

6. ^{d}utu-ra an-še$_3$ šu ba-e-zig$_3$-ge-en-ze$_2$-en

---

[48] "Parsing" a verb is when you explain the form of the verb, as I have been doing in the answer key. Write out the verbal base and the tense (*ḫamtu* or *marû*), person (1st person plural, 2nd person singular, and so on), and the function of other grammatical features (is that /-a/ an adjectival marker, or part of the genitive?).

Transliterate, normalize, and translate the following cuneiform:

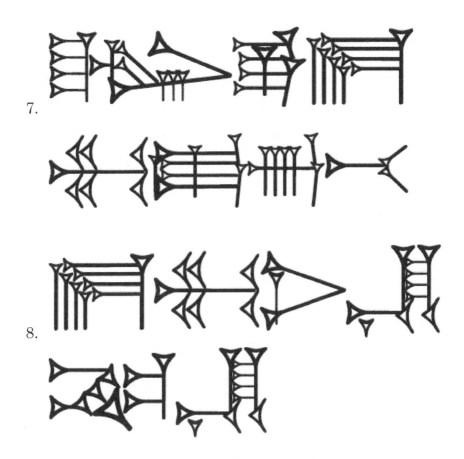

7.

8.

Chapter Eight

Transitive Verbs: *Marû*

We have learned the ways in which the intransitive verb is formed, as well as the transitive verb in the past tense (*ḫamtu*). This leaves us with the transitive present/future tense (*marû*), which is formed with special *endings*. Fortunately for us, these endings are very similar to the intransitive endings:

Sumerian	Person	English
/-en/	1st singular	
i₃-la₂-en		I will hang
/-en/	2nd singular	
i₃-la₂-en		You will hang
/-e/	3rd singular	
i₃-la₂-e		He will hang
/-enden/	1st plural	
i₃-la₂-en-de₃-en		We will hang
/-enzen/	2nd plural	
i₃-la₂-en-ze₂-en		You will hang
/-ene/	3rd plural	
i₃-la₂-e-ne		They will hang

You will notice very quickly that the only differences between these endings and those of the intransitive are the 3rd singular and 3rd plural. The good news is that you have already essentially learned these 3rd person forms. In Chapter Five, you learned that the ending /-e/ indicates the *marû* (for example, /i$_3$-la$_2$-e/), so this form should be very familiar already. In addition, the 3rd plural ending /-ene/ is the same as the plural marker /-ene/, so associating it with the 3rd plural *marû* should be relatively easy.

To review, *marû* verbs place the agent marker *after* the verbal base, while *ḫamtu* verbs place the agent marker *before* the verbal base. In other words, in the *marû* verbal form /i$_3$-la$_2$-e/, the /-e/ tells the reader that the agent is a 3rd person singular "he/she", while in the *ḫamtu* the 3rd singular agent would appear /mu-un-du$_3$/.

Direct Objects in the Verbal Chain

Sumerian can add either a prefix or a suffix to the verbal chain to mark the direct object. The forms are different for the *ḫamtu* and *marû* conjugations:

Person	*Ḫamtu*	*Marû*
1st sg.	/mu-un-du$_3$-en/	/i$_3$-in-la$_2$-e/
2nd sg.	/mu-un-du$_3$-en/	/i$_3$-in-la$_2$-e/

3rd sg. an.	/mu-un-du$_3$-ø/	/i$_3$-in-la$_2$-e/
3rd sg. in.	/mu-un-du$_3$-ø/	/i$_3$-ib-la$_2$-e/
1st pl.	/mu-un-du$_3$-en-de$_3$-en/	???
2nd pl.	/mu-un-du$_3$-en-ze$_2$-en/	???
3rd pl.	/mu-un-du$_3$-eš/	/i$_3$-ne-la$_2$-e/

Let's take a look at the differences between these two paradigms. As the *ḫamtu* verbs use letters before the verbal base to indicate the subject of a sentence, that "slot" is already filled, so the direct object marker must be placed elsewhere. Instead, when it appears, it is placed *after* the verbal base. For example, if we wanted to write "he carried you", it would appear in the form /mu-un-de$_6$-en/, where the /n/ before the verbal base marks the 3rd person agent, and the /-en/ indicates the 2nd person ("you") direct object.

The opposite is true for the *marû*, which marks subjects after the verbal base, so the direct object is placed before it. Unfortunately, in the *marû* singular, the /n/ direct object marker could represent "me", "you", or "him/her", depending on the context. The 3rd person inanimate direct object marker is the only distinct form, as it uses a /b/ instead of an /n/.

Vocabulary

a₂	arm, power
a₂—aŋ̃₂	to command
ŋ̃eštin	wine, vine
ḫul₂	to rejoice
kal	rare, valuable
kaskal	road, journey
ki—us₂	to set (firmly) on the ground; establish
maš₂	goat
maškim	administrator
me	divine power
mes	hero
mu	name, text, year
šu—dab₅	to capture
šu—gid₂	to examine (extispicy)
šu—mu₂	to pray
šu—niŋ̃in	to make a round trip

Cuneiform Signs

kaskal

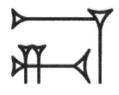

us$_2$

aĝ$_2$

bu

sud

 Ur-Nammu

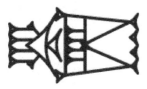

alan

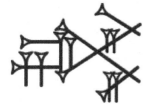

he₂

igi

Exercises

Normalize and translate the sentences, and parse the verbs:

1. e₂ mu-ub-du₃-en

2. kaskal-la g̃eštin mu-de₂-en-de₃-en

3. ᵈinanna šu-ni-še₃ me mu-la₂-e

4. lugal-e kur-ra mu-ni mu-g̃a₂-g̃a₂

5. lu₂-e e₂ dig̃ir-ra-ke₄ ki mu-us₂-e

Transliterate, normalize, and translate the following cuneiform:

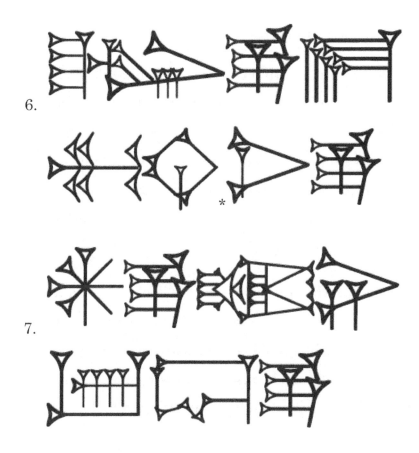

6.

7.

*The second sign in the second line of number six is /ub/.

Chapter Nine

Remaining Verbal Prefixes

Finally! We're going to find out what the /mu-/, /i₃-/, or /ba-/ at the beginning of every verbal form are! If you've been frustrated, we can't blame you; having to ignore certain grammatical elements when learning a new language can be annoying. But the time has come – after this chapter, you will know all of the major parts of the Sumerian verbal chain!

In keeping with the stated goal of this book, this chapter will provide you with only the essentials for understanding the most common verbal prefixes. There are many nuances and a variety of less-common forms that we will cover in the intermediate and advanced books in this series. For now, as always, let's keep things simple.

There are basically two types of prefixes that will show up at the very beginning of a Sumerian verbal chain: a conjugation prefix and a modal prefix. Every verb requires a conjugation prefix, and each conjugation prefix can give you clues as to the type of verb that will be in the chain. Modal prefixes, however, will affect the meaning of the verb itself. For example, the modal prefix /nu-/ negates the verb; if /mu-un-du₃/ means "he built", then the verb /<u>nu</u>-mu-un-du₃/ means "he did <u>not</u> build". We will discuss the common conjugation and modal prefixes below.

Conjugation Prefixes

There are four common conjugation prefixes: /mu-/, /bi₂-/, /ba-/, and /i₃-/. While it is not essential that you remember the differences between these four prefixes, knowing what kinds of verbs usually appear with them may aid you in translation. Some prefixes, for example, normally appear with transitive verbs, and some with intransitive or passive verbs. Additionally, animate subjects/agents generally appear with certain prefixes, while inanimate subjects usually occur with others.

Take a look at the list below:

Prefix	Animate?	Transitive?
/mu-/	animate	transitive
/bi₂-/		transitive
/ba-/	inanimate	intransitive/passive
/i₃/		usually neutral or intransitive

So, if we see the form /mu-un-VERB/, without knowing anything else about the sentence, we would think that the subject (agent) of the verb is animate (person, deity), and that the verb is likely transitive. Conversely, if we saw the prefix chain /ba-an-VERB/, we would assume that the subject of the verb is inanimate, and the verb is likely going to be intransitive or passive. Thus, these prefixes can give you a place to start when you begin to translate the verb in the sentence.

It is also important to note that, because the prefix /i$_3$-/ is a vowel, it will often be assimilated ("disappear" in the writing system) by surrounding vowels. For example, the verbal form /i$_3$-g̃en/ "he went" can be changed to the form /nu-i$_3$-g̃en/ "he did not go". As /i$_3$-/ appears after a vowel, it will be assimilated into the prefix /nu-/, resulting in the final form /nu-g̃en/.

As you can see, it is not usually necessary to remember that /bi$_2$-/ appears with transitive verbs, because if you see the form /bi$_2$-in-du$_3$/, you will already know that /du$_3$/ means "to build", and that it is a transitive verb. However, it is good to understand (at this stage) that there are general correlations between the conjugation prefix and the type of verb it will normally appear with.

Modal Prefixes

The final type of prefix that you need to learn to translate a Sumerian verbal chain is the modal prefix. As with the conjugation prefixes, there are several forms and nuances of modal prefixes that we will not discuss in this chapter. The ones included here are the most important for the beginner to understand.

The three primary modal prefixes appear below:

Sumerian	English	Meaning
/nu-/	no, not	negative
/ga-/	let me, let us	cohortative
/ḫe₂-/	let him...	precative

/nu-/ Negative

The negative modal prefix /nu-/ changes the meaning of the verb from positive to negative. As noted above, if /mu-un-du₃/ means "he built", then /nu-mu-un-du₃/ would mean "he did not build". It's really as simple as that. It is very important to note that the form /nu-/ does not usually like to appear in that exact form before the prefixes /ba-/ and /bi₂-/. As odd as it may seem, the form /nu-/ will actually change before these prefixes, and appear as /li-/ and /la-/. So, instead of /nu-bi₂-in-du₃/, you will usually see the form /li-bi₂-in-du₃/. Likewise, you usually won't see /nu-ba-g̃en/, but rather /la-ba-g̃en/.

No matter what the form (/nu-/, /li-/, or /la-/), it will not change the translation; each will simply negate the verb.

/ga-/ Cohortative

When you see the modal prefix /ga-/, begin by translating it "let me" (if singular) or "let us" (if plural). So, if you see /ga-mu-g̃ar/, you would translate "let me set...". As with the prefix /nu-/, /ga-/ can sometimes change its shape, depending on what follows. The form /ga-mu-g̃ar/ could also appear /gu$_2$-mu-g̃ar/, where the /a/ vowel is "colored" by the /u/ of the /mu-/ prefix. Similarly, if it appears before /bi$_2$-/, it may be written as /gi$_4$-bi$_2$-.../.

Another important aspect of the cohortative prefix /ga-/ is the effect that it has on the rest of the verb. First, the singular will always use the *ḫamtu* form of the verb. The subject of the sentence ("I") is indicated by the /ga-/, so there is no need to write it again before the verbal base, like we normally would. Because of that, a /b/ or /n/ will often appear before the verbal base, indicating the *object*, <u>not the subject</u> of the sentence.

For example, if we saw the form /mu-ub-g̃ar/, we would want understand it to be a *ḫamtu* 3rd singular inanimate (marked by the /b/ before the verbal base) and translate it "it set/placed..." However, if you see the form /ga-mu-ub-g̃ar/, the /b/ before the verbal base is not marking the subject of the verb; it is marking the *direct object*. Think about it like this: the /ga-/ tells you that it is a 1st person subject, so you don't need another marker. Because a /ga-/ has been placed at the front of the verb, it is "pulling" the marker of the direct object from being at the end of the verbal chain to the position before the verb.

/ḫe₂-/ Precative

The final prefix that we will investigate in this chapter is the precative, which (for now) is to be translated "let him/her/it...", or "may he/she/it...". Thus, if /mu-du₃-e/ means "he will build", then /ḫe₂-mu-du₃-e/ would be translated "<u>Let</u> him build".[49] As with the other modal prefixes, the form /ḫe₂-/ can vary depending on the conjugation prefix that follows. If followed by /ba-/, you will often see /<u>ḫa</u>-ba-.../. Likewise, if followed by /mu-/, it will often be written with the form /<u>ḫu</u>-mu-.../.

Vocabulary

abzu	Abzu
alim	bison
a-nun-na	Anuna gods

---

[49]The precative, as expected, can be far more nuanced in meaning than a simple precative. We will discuss these nuances in a later volume of this series.

bur-^{d}en-zu	Bur-Suen
^{d}dumu-zi	Dumuzi
e$_2$-ḫur-saĝ	Eḫursaĝ temple
e$_2$-kur	Ekur temple
e$_2$-maḫ	Emaḫ temple
e-ne	he, she
lamma	figurine deity
me-lim$_4$	frightening splendor
men	crown, tiara
ne-saĝ	first-fruit offering
ni$_2$	fear
nindaba	(food) offering
^{gi}pisaĝ	reed basket
sed$_4$	(to be) cold

Cuneiform Signs

za

geme$_2$

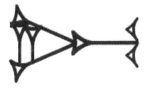

gu

el

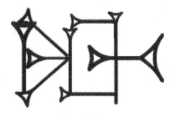

dam

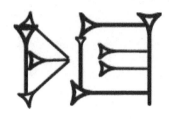 nin

 saĝ

 gid₂

Bau (ᵈba-u₂)

Exercises

Normalize and translate the sentences, and parse the verbs:

1. lugal e₂-kur-še₃ nu-g̃en

2. e-ne ᵍⁱpisag̃ ḫe₂-tum₃

3. dig̃ir lugal-še₃ me-lim₄-a-ni mu-un-šum₂

4. ᵈen-ki lugal abzu-ke₄ ba-an-du₁₁

5. ᵈen-lil₂-ra šu ga-na-mu₂

Transliterate, normalize, and translate the following cuneiform:

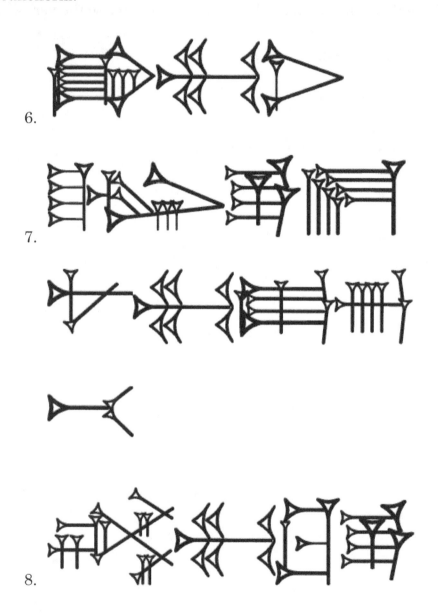

6.

7.

8.

Chapter Ten

Compound and Auxiliary Verbs

Compound Verbs

Sometimes in English, we find that forming a verb with a single word is not enough to say exactly what we mean. In these cases, we often add another word to the verb (like an adjective, adverb, or even a noun) to complement the verb. For example, if you write a draft of a book – say, a Sumerian grammar – and give it to someone to read through and edit, that person is "proofreading" the manuscript. The word "read" is not enough to specify what that person will do with the manuscript. A preliminary or trial version of a document is known as a "proof", so we add the word "proof" to the verb "read" to make a type of "compound" verb. Other examples include "color-code", "daydream", and "kickstart". Sumerian does something similar, as they will often combine a verb and a noun, which functions as a direct object of the verb. Let me give you some examples (many of which you have already learned):

Sumerian	English
gu₃—de₂	to speak (literally, "to pour out (de₂) the voice (gu₃)")
igi—g̃ar:	to look at (literally, "to place (g̃ar) the eye (igi)")
sag̃—il₂:	to raise (il₂) the head (sag̃)
sag̃—gid₂:	to become angry (literally, "to lengthen (gid₂) the (fore)head (sag̃)")

Notice that in each of these examples there is a verbal component (/de₂/, /g̃ar/, /il₂/, /gid₂/) and a noun that is the direct object of that verb (/gu₃/, /igi/, /sag̃/). In other words, the first part of the compound verb (the noun) will always be the grammatical object of the verbal component, and never the subject/agent (for example, the verb /igi—g̃ar/ will never be understood "the eye (subject) sets [X]"; it will always be "[X] sets the eye (object)").

We have learned that direct objects in Sumerian sentences have no specific marks to identify them as direct objects; we say that they are marked with a "zero" (ø). Thus, if we were to "normalize" the sentence /lugal-e gu₃ bi₂-in-de₂/ "the king spoke", we would write it like this:

lugal.e gu$_3$.ø bi$_2$.n.de$_2$.ø

How do we explain what's going on in this sentence, grammatically?

-the /.e/ on /lugal/ represents the *ergative*, marking it as the *agent*

-the /gu$_3$/ is the noun component of the compound verb, and the /.ø/ on /gu$_3$/ is the mark of the *direct object*, which is paralleled in the verb with /.ø/

-/bi$_2$/ is the *conjugation prefix*

-/n/ before /de$_2$/ is the marker for the 3rd person *agent* (cross-referencing the *ergative* /.e/*)

-/de$_2$/ is the verbal part of the compound verb

At this point, most or all of the analysis above should make sense to you. But this leads to a slight complication: what do you do if your compound verb itself needs a direct object (called the oblique object)? For example, the compound verb /igi—du$_8$/ means "to look at". How do you mark the direct object of a verb that already has a direct object in it? There are generally three ways that Sumerian marks this *oblique object*:

1. Locative-terminative /e/

   /g̃eštin-e šu ba-an-ti/   he received
   wine

2. Locative /a/

   /er₂-ra šu ba-an-ti/   he received
   (his) tears [er₂]

3. No marking

   /dub šu ba-an-ti/   he received the
   tablet

Auxiliary Verbs

Compound verbs can also appear in a somewhat odd construction, in which the two parts of the compound verb appear *before* the verbal chain, and either the verb /ak/ ("to do") or /du₁₁/ ("to say") is *in* the verbal chain. The construction usually looks like this:

/e₂ ki us₂ mu-ak-e/   "he will firmly
establish the house"

From this example, we notice several things. First, the verb /ak/ appears in the verbal chain, while the compound verb /ki—us₂/ comes directly before the verbal chain. The meaning of the verb has not changed, but instead of writing the verb

/ki mu-us$_2$-e/, they used an auxiliary verb (/ak/) in the verbal chain (/ki us$_2$ mu-ak-e/). As noted above, the auxiliary verb that is written in the verbal chain can appear either as /ak/ or /du$_{11}$/, and although the verb is written quite differently, we are not yet aware of the nuanced meaning of this verbal construction.

Vocabulary

^{d}ba-u$_2$	Bau
^{d}inanna	Inanna
lipiš	inner body, heart, anger
me—teš$_2$	to praise
mi$_2$	praise
mir	to be angry
mul	star; to shine
muš	snake
nar	musician
ne$_3$	strength, force
ni$_2$ (II)[50]	self
^{d}nin-g̃ir$_2$-su	Ningirsu
pa—e$_3$	to cause to appear
saḫ$_2$	pig
sag$_9$	to be good, beautiful
šul-gi	Šulgi
siskur$_2$	prayer, offering
ša$_3$—ḫul$_2$	to be happy

---

[50] If you think this looks familiar, you're right – many Sumerian words have multiple meanings. /ni$_2$/ can mean "fear" (as you've already seen), as well as "self".

Cuneiform Signs

ib

la$_2$

diš

šum$_2$

in

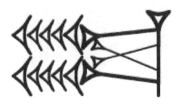

tu

pi

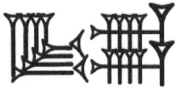

sa₆

g̃ar

Exercises

Normalize and translate the sentences, and parse the verbs:

1. ur-sag̃ ša₃ nu-ḫul₂

2. gu₃-de₂-a maš₂-a šu i₃-gid₂ maš₂-a-ni i₃-sag₉

3. lugal-e siskur₂-ra-na šu ba-an-ti

4. nin-e nam-maḫ-a-ni⁵¹ pa e₃ bi₂-in-ak

---

⁵¹ /-ni/ can also be read as /-ne₂/

Transliterate, normalize, and translate the following cuneiform:

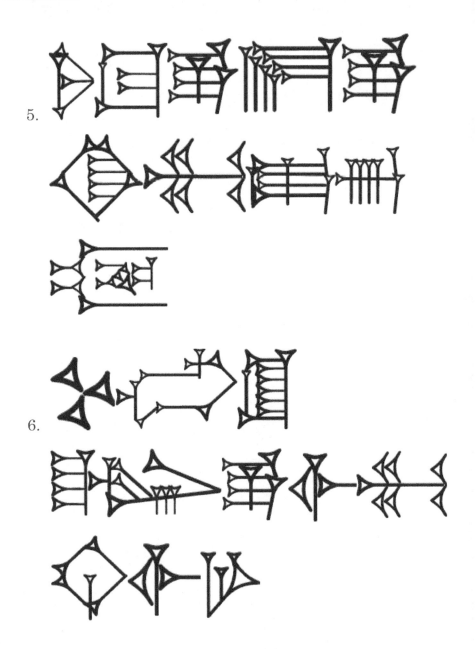

5.

6.

Chapter Eleven

Imperatives and Several Non-Finite Forms

Imperatives

There are many times in life that we need to tell people what to do. If we need our son Johnny to clean up his room, we can't very well walk into his room and say to him, "Johnny will clean up his room". Well, I suppose we could, but we would only get a confused look from him. English has a specific way to form a "command" sentence: "(Johnny) clean up your room".

The same is true in Sumerian; there is a specific form that is used to give commands, which we call the "imperative". The form is actually quite simple: it is formed on the *ḫamtu* singular base (even in the plural), and the verbal base will *move to the front* of the verbal chain. The verbal chain will either be deleted, replaced with (usually) an /a/ vowel, or slightly modified.

Let's look at a couple of examples. If /šum$_2$/ means "to give", the imperative could simply be written /šum$_2$-ma/ "give!" (appearing in the same form as the participle). Very often, however, the verbal chain remains, but is slightly modified.

Thus, if the form /mu-šum₂/ means "you gave (it)", the imperative would be /šum₂-ma-ab/ "give it!" Without worrying about the /-ma-ab/ for the moment, you quickly notice that the /šum₂/ has been moved from its normal position near the end of the verbal chain to the very beginning. This is the essence of the form of the imperative.

As for the /-ma-ab/, one of the odd features of the imperative is that a vowel may appear in the verbal chain that we would not expect; it is often an /a/ vowel. So, instead of seeing the form /šum₂-mu-ub/, we see /šum₂-ma-ab/. This only leaves the /b/ to be explained, and you can probably guess what it represents: the 3ʳᵈ person inanimate object ("it").

Another example can be seen in the imperative form /du₁₁-ga-na-ab/ "Say it to him!" Let's examine this from left to right: /du₁₁/ = verbal base, with a /g/ auslaut, followed by the /a/ vowel; /na/ is the standard 3ʳᵈ person dative; /b/ in /ab/ is the 3ʳᵈ person inanimate object. The most important thing to remember with the imperative is that the verbal base will move *to the front* of the verbal chain, and it will usually be followed by some sort of /a/ vowel, and maybe a verbal chain.

Non-Finite Forms

Non-finite simply refers to those forms that are not "regular" verbs (infinitives, participles, etc.). We learned in an earlier lesson that the verbal form can appear by itself (or with an /a/) and be translated as either a passive way (/šum₂-ma/ "given" or /ĝar-ra/ "set, placed"), or like a participle (usually ending in /-ing/ in English: /du₁₁-ga/ "saying" and /ĝar-ra/ "placing"). Without going into too much detail at this point, we need to know about two basic forms: the *ḫamtu* and *marû* participles.

We just discussed the *ḫamtu* participle, which will usually be the verbal base followed by an /a/ vowel, and is often a passive participle. The *marû* participle, however, is the active participle in Sumerian. It is formed with the *marû* verbal base, followed by an /e(d)/.[52] Like the writing of the genitive /ak/, the *marû* participle's /e(d)/ will appear in different ways depending on the form of the verbal base. It is not necessary to discuss the variety of forms at this point, but if you see a *marû* verb with no verbal chain, followed by /e/, or with a /d/ followed by a vowel (/a/, /e/, or even /am/), you are likely looking at a *marû* participle.

Sumerian	Normalization
-/gi₄-gi₄/[53]	/gi₄.gi₄.e(d)

---

[52] The specific meaning of the *marû* participle is still debated, along with some details on its form; we will deal with it in greater detail in a later grammar.
[53] There is no /e/ here, as the verb ends in a vowel.

-/šum$_2$-m<u>u</u>/	/šum$_2$.e(d)/
-/tar-r<u>e</u>-<u>de</u>$_3$/	/tar.ede/
-/tar-r<u>e</u>-<u>da</u>/	/tar.ede/
-/tar-r<u>e</u>-<u>dam</u>/	/tar.edam/

The specific meaning of the *marû* participle is sometimes unclear or debated, but for our purposes, the best way to translate it (initially) is either like an active participle ("the one who...") or as a purpose clause ("in order to...".). So, if you see /en nam tar-re-de$_3$/ normalized as /en nam tar.ede/, you would begin by translating it "the lord who decides fates". If this translation did not fit the context, you would translate it either "the lord, in order to decide the fate..." Similarly, if you see /e$_2$ du$_3$-de$_3$/ (/e$_2$ du$_3$.ede/; the first /e/ of /-ede/ does not appear after a vowel), you would initially translate this "the one who builds the house". If this does not work in the context, you might try, "in order to build the house..."

Subordinate Constructions

When we say, "Johnny, who is wearing the red shirt, is coming with us to the park", the phrase "the boy who is wearing the red shirt" is a "subordinate" or "dependent" clause. If we were to remove it, the sentence would still make sense; the clause serves to tell us more about something found in the main sentence. In this case, it tells us more about Johnny.

While we will deal with the different ways in which Sumerian can form subordinate clauses in our second book in this series, it would be a good idea to breifly mention one very common construction here: the /lu$_2$...a/ construction. We know that /lu$_2$/ means "man," but but it can also just mean "a man" or "individual." The /a/ at the end essentially tells us where the dependent or subordinate clause *stops*. If we were to insert it into our English sentence above, it would look something like this: "Johnny, /lu$_2$/ ("the individual who") is wearing the red shirt /a/, is coming with us to the park."

As you can see, the /lu$_2$/ and /a/ essentially mark the beginning and end of the subordinate clause. So, if we read the sentence, /lugal i$_3$-gub/ "the king stood," we can add a subordinate clause to it: /lugal lu$_2$-e e$_2$ mu-un-du$_3$-a i$_3$-gub/ "The king, the one who built the temple, stood." Notice that the /lu$_2$/ stands at the beginning of the clause, and the /a/ marks the end, so that the reader knows exactly where the dependent or subordinate clause begins and ends.

Vocabulary

e-ne—du$_{11}$	to play
ḫul$_2$	to rejoice
luḫ	to clean, wash
lul	untrue, false, criminal
mar-tu	westerner
me-a	where?
me-še$_3$	where to?
mi$_2$—du$_{11}$	to care for, treat well
mu$_4$	to get dressed
nam—ku$_4$	to curse
pad$_3$	to find
raḫ$_2$	to beat, kill
sag$_3$	to beat, strike
sal	thin, fine
sar (I)	to write
sar (II)	to run, hasten

Cuneiform Signs

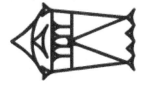

na$_2$

pad$_3$

u$_4$

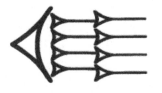

mi

ul

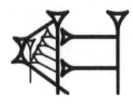

ka

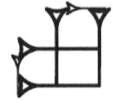

uru

Exercises

Normalize and translate the sentences, and parse the verbs:

1. lugal-ra du$_{11}$-ga-ab

2. nin-ra maš$_2$ šum$_2$-mu-na-ab

3. ^{d}en-ki en nam tar-tar-re-de$_3$

4. e$_2$ du$_3$-de$_3$ e$_2$ ki us$_2$-se-de$_3$

5. lugal lu$_2$ e$_2$-še$_3$ ba-g̃en-a i$_3$-gub

Transliterate, normalize, and translate the following cuneiform:

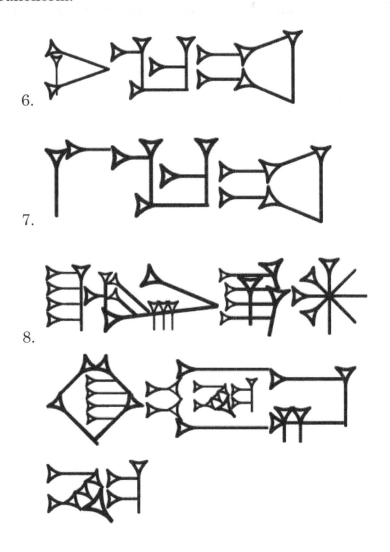

6.

7.

8.

Conclusion

Congratulations! You have taken a giant step toward reading ancient Sumerian with proficiency! Although this book is designed to be an elementary-level grammar, if the grammatical principles, vocabulary, and signs found here are mastered, you will be able to translate a great deal of Sumerian.

In the following appendices, you will find study tools, along with a series of exercises that are intended to put your newfound knowledge to the test. There are Sumerian readings in transliteration from several genres, including royal inscriptions, literature, and year names, as well as drawings of real cuneiform tablets, focusing primarily on the genre of royal inscriptions – there's nothing quite as exciting as translating directly from an object that's 4,000 years old!

When new or variant grammatical concepts are found in these exercises, short explanations will be provided to make reading possible.

It is our recommendation that you take your time and thoroughly understand the concepts presented in this book before moving on to the intermediate volume (forthcoming).

Memorize the vocabulary, learn to recognize the signs, and master the grammatical principles. If you have questions or need help, please do not hesitate to contact us at Digital Hammurabi! Contact details can be found on our website, www.digitalhammurabi.com.

We are so excited that you have begun this journey with us!

Appendix A

Additional Exercises

Royal Inscriptions[54]

Normalize and translate. Additional vocabulary can be found in Appendix C.

Inscription 1.

^{d}ba-u$_2$

munus sag$_9$-ga

dumu an-na

nin uru ku$_3$-ga

nin-a-ni

gu$_3$-de$_2$-a

ensi$_2$

lagaš^{ki}-ke$_4$

e$_2$ uru ku$_3$-ga-ka-ni

mu-na-du$_3$

---

[54] All of the inscriptions here are taken from the series *The Royal Inscriptions of Mesopotamia*, often referred to as "RIME". A full list of inscriptional references can be found in Appendix H.

Inscription 2

^{d}en-lil$_2$

lugal diĝir-re-ne-ra

eš$_3$ nibru^{ki}

dur-an-ki-še$_3$

gu$_3$-de$_2$-a

ensi$_2$

lagaš^{ki}

ma$_2$-gid$_2$

e$_2$-kur-ra-ke$_4$

nam-ti-la-ni-še$_3$

a mu-na-ru

Inscription 3

^{d}inanna

nin kur-kur-ra

nin-a-ni

gu$_3$-de$_2$-a

ensi$_2$

lagaš^{ki}

ur ^{d}ĝa$_2$-tum$_3$-du$_{10}$-ke$_4$

e$_2$-an-na ĝir$_2$-su^{ki}-ka-ni

mu-na-du$_3$

Inscription 4

^{d}inanna

nin kur-kur-ra

nin-a-ni

gu$_3$-de$_2$-a

ensi$_2$

lagaš^{ki}-ke$_4$

e$_2$-an-na g̃ir$_2$-su^{ki}-ka-ni

mu-na-du$_3$

Inscription 5

^{d}nin-a-zu

dig̃ir-ra-ni

gu$_3$-de$_2$-a

ensi$_2$

lagaš^{ki}-ke$_4$

e$_2$ g̃ir$_2$-su^{ki}-ka-ni

mu-na-du$_3$

Inscription 6

^{d}nin-g̃ir$_2$-su

ur-sag̃ kala-ga

^{d}en-lil$_2$-la$_2$-ra

gu$_3$-de$_2$-a

ensi$_2$

lagaš^{ki}-ke$_4$

niĝ$_2$-du$_7$-e pa mu-na-e$_3$

e$_2$-ninnu anzu$_2$^{mušen} babbar$_2$-ra-ni

mu-na-du$_3$

Inscription 7

^{d}nin-ĝir$_2$-su

ur-saĝ kala-ga

^{d}en-lil$_2$-la$_2$

lugal-a-ni

gu$_3$-de$_2$-a

ensi$_2$

lagaš^{ki}-ke$_4$

e$_2$-ba-gara$_2$-ka-ni

mu-na-du$_3$

Inscription 8

^{d}nin-sumun$_2$

diĝir-ra-ni

ur-^{d}nammu

nita kala-ga

lugal uri₅^{ki}-ma

lugal ki-en-gi ki-uri-ke₄

e₂-maḫ

e₂ ki aĝ₂-ĝa₂-ni

mu-na-du₃

Inscription 9

ur-^{d}nammu

lugal uri₅^{ki}-ma

lugal ki-en-gi ki-uri

lu₂ e₂ ^{d}en-lil₂-la₂

in-du₃-a

Inscription 10

^{d}en-lil₂

lugal kur-kur-ra

lugal-a-ni

ur-^{d}nammu

nita kala-ga

lugal uri₅^{ki}-ma

lugal ki-en-gi ki-uri-ke₄

e₂-kur

e₂ ki ag̃₂-g̃a₂-ni

mu-na-du₃

Inscription 11

ᵈinanna

nin-a-ni-ir

ᵈ*bur*-ᵈen-zu

lugal kala-ga

lugal ki-en-gi ki-uri

mu-na-dim₂

nam-ti-la-ni-še₃

a mu-na-ru

Inscription 12

ᵈbur-ᵈen-zu

lugal kala-ga

lugal ki-en-gi ki-uri

ab-ba-mu

dub-sar

dumu lu₂-ᵈutu

ir₃-zu

Year Names[55]

Using your knowledge of Sumerian, translate the year names below. They take the format "Year X happened".

1. mu šul-gi lugal

2. mu g̃iri₃ nibru^{ki} si bi₂-sa₂

3. mu e₂-ḫur-sag̃ lugal ba-du₃

4. mu ^{g̃iš}na₂ ^dnin-lil₂-la₂ ba-dim₂

5. mu bad₃-an^{ki} ba-ḫul

6. mu us₂-sa bad₃-an^{ki} ba-ḫul

7. mu ^dšul-gi lugal-e bad₃ ma-da mu-du₃

Translations from Cuneiform

This section contains a selection of hand copies, all of royal inscriptions. "Hand copies" are line-drawings of cuneiform made by Assyriologists for easy reading. Cuneiform can be tricky to see in photographs, so hand copies are often made for publication purposes – either to illustrate a new text so

---

55 All of these are year names of the Mesopotamian king, Šulgi, who was a member of the Ur III dynasty and reigned during the 21st century B.C.E. From Sigrist and Gomi, 1991.

others can translate it, or so that other people can check your translation by reading the drawing of the cuneiform. These hand copies were created based on existing hand copies and photographs found on the Cuneiform Digital Library Initiative (CDLI) database. If you want to see the original copies, and get some more information about these inscriptions, just enter their 'P' number into the CDLI database search-bar![56]

Transliterate[57], normalize, and translate these texts. Check the vocabulary and sign glossaries for any signs or words you don't recognize.

---

[56] Search for "CDLI" in the search engine of your choice to find CDLI. Enter the P number in the search field names "CDLI no." and hit "search"!

[57] Write out the cuneiform signs as you see them.

Hand Copy 1, P226644

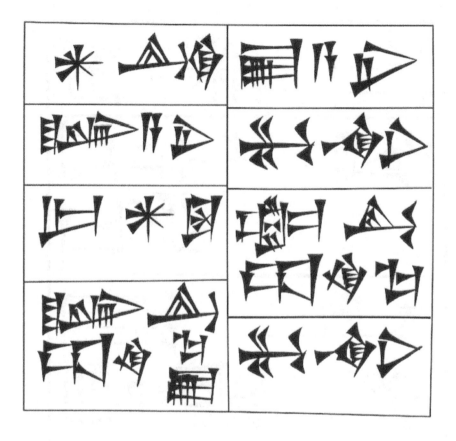

Hand Copy 2, P226818

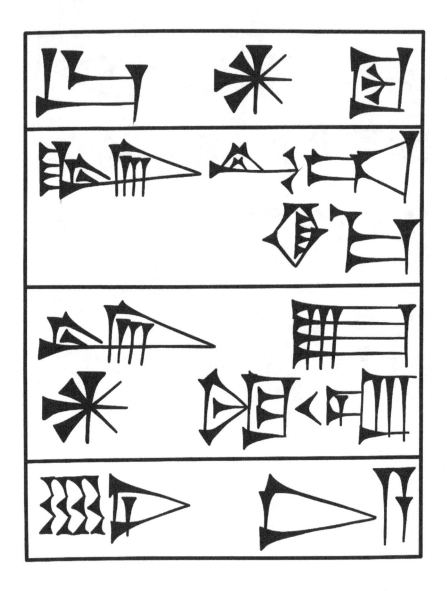

Hand Copy 3, P232332 (double-sided inscription)

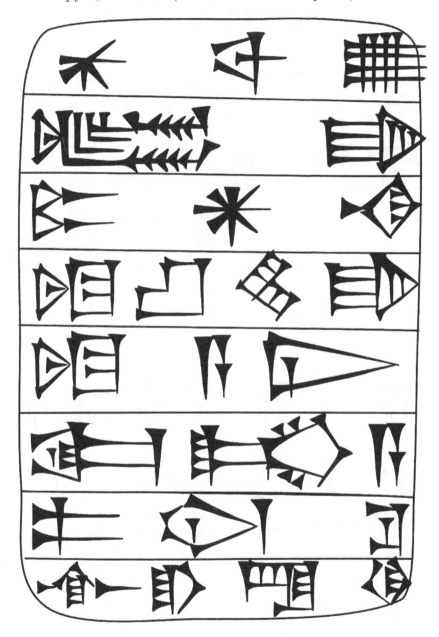

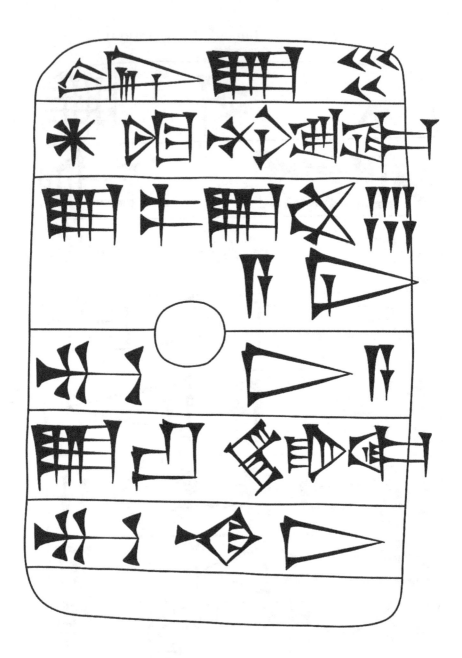

Hand Copy 4, P226202

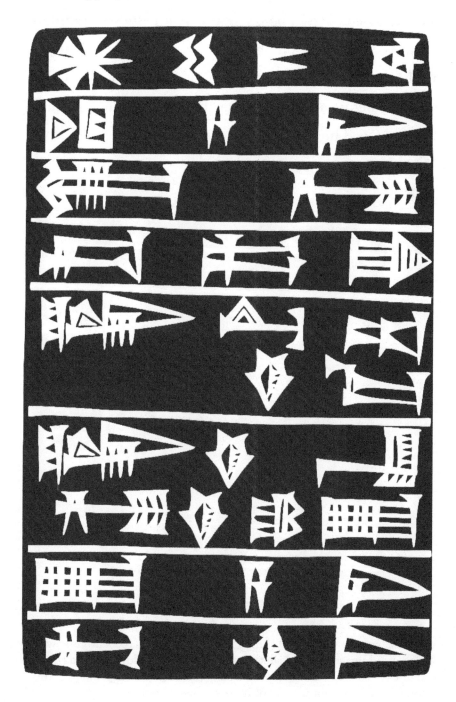

For additional cuneiform translation practice, use CDLI to look up the objects listed below. They will include unfamiliar signs and vocabulary! Don't be intimidated, you can do it! The CDLI entries all include transliterations to help you identify new signs, and you can use the ePSD to look up new vocabulary. Good luck![58]

P216646

P226876

P226639

P226707

P227153

P226829

P232309

P232314

P232338

P232424

---

[58] Remember, search for "ePSD Sumerian" to locate ePSD. Put your word into the search bar, selection "Dictionary" in the drop-down bar to the left, and click "GO". Not sure how to write š, ḫ, or ĝ? Not a problem! The ePSD homepage has a handy set of instructions to help you out.

Appendix B

Answer Key

Lesson One

1. e₂

   /e₂/

   "house"

2. lugal

   /lugal/

   "king"

3. lugal maḫ

   /lugal maḫ/

   "magnificent king"

   We know that /lugal/ means "king," and /maḫ/ is an adjective that means "magnificent," and adjectives come after nouns in Sumerian.

4. nin

   /nin/

   "lady"

5. dub-sar

/dub.sar/

"scribe"

6. dub-sar-re-ne

/dub.sar.ene/

"scribes"

We know that a /dub.sar/ is a "scribe," but what does
the /-re-ne/ mean? The /r/ on /-re/ connects the ending
/.ene/ to /dub.sar/, which ends in /r/.

7. kur

/kur/

"mountain"

8. lugal gal-gal

/lugal gal.gal/

"great kings"

The adjective /gal/ means "big, great," and when an
adjective is reduplicated, it makes the noun that it
modifies plural.

9. nita$_2$ kala-ga

/nita$_2$ kala.a/

"mighty man"

The noun /nita$_2$/ "man" is modified by the adjective
/kala/ "mighty." Remember, /kala/ has a /g/ auslaut, so

the /g/ in /-ga/ comes from /kala(g)/, leaving an /a/ suffix, which marks the adjective.

10. me₃ gal-gal-la

   /me₃ gal.gal.a/

   "great battles"

   The adjective /gal/ is reduplicated, and has the marker /a/ for the adjective.

11. ḫur-saḡ

   /ḫur.saḡ/

   "mountain"

12. kur gal-la

   /kur gal.a/

   "big mountain"

   The word /kur/ "mountain" is modified by the adjective /gal/ "big," which is marked with the marker of the adjective /a/.

13. e₂ maḫ

   /e₂ maḫ/

   "magnificent house"

   The adjective /maḫ/ "magnificent" modifies the noun /e₂/ "house."

14. kur-kur

/kur.kur/

"mountains"

When a noun is reduplicated, it expresses plurality.

15. dumu-e-ne

/dumu.ene/

"sons"

The noun /dumu/ "son" has the ending /-e-ne/ attached to it, making it plural.

16. dumu tur

/dumu tur/

"young son"

The noun /dumu/ "son" is modified by /tur/ "small, young."

17. diĝir

/diĝir/

"god"

18. diĝir-re-ne

/diĝir.ene/

"gods"

The noun /diĝir/ "god" contains the suffix /.ene/ (plural marker).

19. ur-saĝ kala-ga

    /ur.saĝ kala.a/

    "mighty hero"

    The noun /ur-saĝ/ "hero" is modified by the adjective /kala/, which contains the adjective marker /a/.

20. ama gal

    /ama gal/

    "great mother"

    The noun /ama/ "mother" is modified by the adjective /gal/.

21. lugal

    "king"

22. nin maḫ

    "magnificent lady"

23. diĝir gal

    "great god"

Lesson Two

1. e₂ lugal-la

   /e₂ lugal.ak/

   "the house of the king"

   The noun /e₂/ "house" is followed by another noun,

/lugal/ "king." When two nouns follow one another, we often find them to be connected by the genitive marker /-ak/. Because /lugal/ ends in a consonant, that final consonant /l/ is used to connect the genitive marker /-ak/ to /lugal/. Because nothing follows the genitive marker, and the /k/ of the genitive will not stand by itself at the end of a word, the /k/ drops out, leaving the form /e₂ lugal-la/.

2. bad₃ gal

   /bad₃ gal/

   "big wall"

   The noun /bad₃/ "wall" is modified by the adjective /gal/ "big."

3. nig̃₂ šum₂-ma

   /nig̃₂ šum₂.a/

   "a given thing"

   We see immediately that an /a/ is attached to the word /šum₂/. Because /šum₂/ is a verb ("to give"), we know that this /a/ likely marks a participle, which we would translate either as a verb ending in /-ing/ ("giving"), or as a passive ("given"), which makes better sense here.

4. dig̃ir-ra-ni

   /dig̃ir.ani/

"his/her god"

The ending /.ani/ is the 3rd person possessive suffix "his/her." The /r/ on the syllable /ra/ duplicates the final consonant on /diĝir/.

5. e₂ lugal-la mu-un-du₃

/e₂ lugal.ak mu.n.du₃/

"He built the house of the king"

As we have not yet learned how to translate verbs, simply read /mu-un-du₃/ as "he built." As above, /e₂ lugal-la/ represents /e₂ lugal.ak/, and /du₃/ means "to build." Notice that the verb comes at the end of the sentence.

6. ki-aĝ₂-ĝa₂

/ki.aĝ₂.a/

"beloved (one)"

The verb /ki—aĝ₂/ means "to love," and the /ĝ/ on the syllable /ĝa₂/ tells us that /a/ should be attached to the end of the verb. When an /a/ appears at the end of a verb, we often translate it as a participle, either with /-ing/ ("loving") or as a passive ("beloved (one)").

7. ensi₂ ki-en-gi ki-uri-ke₄

/ensi₂ ki.en.gi ki.uri.ak.e/

"The ruler of Sumer and Akkad"

As we have not yet learned what that final /e/ might mean, just ignore it for the moment. You will notice that the noun /ensi₂/ "ruler" is followed by two other nouns, /ki-en-gi/ "Sumer" and /ki-uri/ "Akkad." The /k/ at the end of /ki-uri/ is the genitive /-ak/, and since it follows a word that ends in a vowel, and has something written after it, you see the /k/ of /-ak/ written, but not the /a/. It is also interesting to note that only one genitive /-ak/ is needed for both "Sumer" and "Akkad."

8. lugal-la e₂-ni

   /lugal.ak e₂.ani/

   "The house of the king."

   This is the "anticipatory genitive" construction that we talked about, where instead of saying "the house of the king," they write, "Of the king, his house." The /a/ on /lugal/ is the genitive, while the /-ni/ on /e₂/ represents /.ani/. The /a/ does not appear, as it comes after a vowel.

9. dumu lugal-la

   /dumu lugal.ak/

   "The son of the king"

   This is a straightforward genitive construction. The /l/

in /la/ is the auslaut of /lugal/, and the /a/ represents the genitive marker /-ak/.

10. dumu gal-la lugal-la

/dumu gal.a lugal.ak/

"the great son of the king"

More genitives, but this time with a bonus adjective! The /la/ attached to /gal/ is the auslaut with the adjectival marker /a/, while the /la/ attached to /lugal/ is the auslaut with the genitive marker /-ak/.

11. e₂ digir-ra

/e₂ digir.ak/

"The house of the god"

Again, the /ra/ contains the auslaut of /digir/ and the /a/ of the genitive marker /-ak/.

12. dumu lugal-la

/dumu lugal.ak/

"The son of the king"

The /la/ contains the /l/ auslaut of /lugal/ and the /a/ of the genitive marker /-ak/.

13. e₂ gal lugal-la

/e₂ gal lugal.ak/

"The great house of the king"

/gal/ is an adjective modifying /e₂/, and (as above) the

/la/ is the /l/ auslaut of /lugal/ and the /a/ from the genitive marker /-ak/.

Lesson Three

1. lu₂-da

   /lu₂.da/

   "With the man"

2. e₂-še₃

   /e₂.še₃/

   "To(ward) the house"

3. a-e ba-diri

   /a.e ba.diri/

   "It floated on the water"

   The verb /diri/ means "to float," and since /a/ means "water," the /e/ is most likely the locative-terminative, which means "on, near, at."

4. lugal e₂-a i₃-g̃en

   /lugal.ø e₂.a i₃.g̃en/

   "The king went into the house"

   If we begin with the verb (without worrying about the /i₃-/ just yet), we know that /g̃en/ means "to go" (an *intransitive* verb). If we look back in the sentence, we see that there is a likely subject for the verb "to go" -

/lugal/ "king." So, if we translate "The king went...", that just leaves us with /e$_2$-a/. We know that /e$_2$/ means "house," and the /a/ is likely the locative case ending, meaning "into."

5. lugal-le e$_2$ mu-du$_3$

    /lugal.e e$_2$.ø mu.du$_3$/

    "The king built the house"

    The /-le/ on /lugal/ is the /e/ of the ergative, and since /du$_3$/ means "to build" (a *transitive* verb), we look for an *agent* (subject of a transitive verb) in the sentence: /lugal/. This just leaves the /e$_2$/, which is the *direct object* of the verb "to build", which is marked with a "zero" /ø/ (absolutive case).

6. ^{d}en-lil$_2$-ra ^{d}nanna bi$_2$-in-du$_{11}$

    /^{d}en.lil$_2$.ra ^{d}nanna.e bi$_2$.na.n.du$_{11}$/

    "Nanna spoke to Enlil"

    Again ignoring the first part of the verb /bi$_2$-in-/ (which turns into the /bi$_2$.na.n/ in the verbal chain), the verb /du$_{11}$/ means "to say, speak," so we begin with the translation "he/she said..." If we look back in the sentence, we see that there is a /-ra/ on the name /^{d}en-lil$_2$/, which is the dative marker "to, for". This leaves /^{d}nanna/ in the sentence as the likely agent of the transitive verb "to say, speak". Even though the ergative marker /e/ is not written, I have represented it in the normalization.

7. uru-ta ^{d}utu i$_3$-g̃en

/uru.ta ^{d}utu.ø i$_3$.g̃en/

"Utu went (away) from the city"

We see the suffix /-ta/ attached to the noun /uru/ "city", letting us know that something is happening "from the city." This leaves /^{d}utu/ as the likely subject, which we mark with a /ø/, since /g̃en/ "to go" is an intransitive verb.

8. lugal-me-en

/lugal.me.en/

"I am the king"

/lugal/ plus the 1st person singular copula /me.en/.

9. dig̃ir ki-en-gi-ra-ak-am$_3$

/dig̃ir ki.en.gi.ak.am$_3$/

"He/She is the god of Sumer"

The syllable /ra/ contains the /r/ auslaut of /gi(r)/. The /ak/ is the genitive marker, and /am$_3$/ is the 3rd person singular copula.

Lesson Four

1. ᵈen-lil₂-e ᵈnin-g̃ir₂-su-še₃ igi mu-ši-bar

   /ᵈen.lil₂.e ᵈnin.g̃ir₂.su.še₃ igi.ø mu.ši.n.bar/

   "Enlil looked at Ningirsu"

   If we begin with the verb /igi—bar/ "to look at," we notice that there is a /-ši-/ in the verbal chain; this tells us to look for a /-še₃/ in the sentence, which we see attached to "Ningirsu." This leaves us with /ᵈen-lil₂-e/, where the ergative marker /e/ is attached to the divine name Enlil, who acts as the agent of the transitive verb.

2. lugal-ra ᵈutu mu-na-du₁₁

   /lugal.ra ᵈutu.e mu.na.n.du₁₁/

   "Utu said to the king"

   The verb /du₁₁/ means "to say, speak," and the dative /-na-/ in the verbal chain tells us to look for a /-ra/ in the sentence, which we find attached to the noun /lugal/. This leaves /ᵈutu/ as the agent of the verb /du₁₁/.

3. lu₂-da mu-un-da-gub

   /lu₂.da mu.n.da.gub/

   "He stood with the man."

   The verb /gub/ "to stand" contains the form /-da-/ in its verbal chain, telling us to look for a /-da/ "with" in the sentence, which we find on the word /lu₂/ "man." The /n/ that appears before the /-da-/ in the verbal chain tells us "with *whom*" the subject is standing. It signals us to look for an animate being with /-da/ attached to it.

4. kalam-ta diĝir mu-ta-ĝen

/kalam.ta diĝir.ø mu.ta.ĝen/

"The god went away from the land."

The ablative /-ta-/ "from" appears in the verbal chain with the verbal base /ĝen/ "to go," which sends us looking for a /-ta/ in the sentence. A /-ta/ is attached to /kalam/, indicating motion *away from* the /kalam/ "land." This leaves /diĝir/ in the sentence, which acts as the subject of the intransitive verb /ĝen/ "to go," which I have marked with a /ø/, indicating that it is the subject of an intransitive verb.

5. lugal-me-en

/lugal.me.en/

"I am/You are the king"

6. lugal-e e₂ mu-un-du₃

/lugal.e e₂.ø mu.n.du₃/

"The king built the temple."

We haven't learned about everything in this sentence

yet, so don't panic – for now, we're ignoring the /n/ in the verbal chain. As the agent of a transitive verb, /lugal/ is in the ergative, as it is the subject of a transitive verb /du₃/. The noun /e₂/ is the direct object of a transitive verb and is marked with /-ø/.

7. diĝir-ra lugal-e e₂ mu-un-na-du₃

/diĝir.ra lugal.e e₂.ø mu.n.na.du₃/

"The king built the temple for the god."

The noun /lugal/ is marked with the ergative as it is the subject of a transitive verb. /diĝir/ is marked with the dative /-ra/, which is linked to the /na/ in the verbal chain, indicating that the temple was built *for* the god.[59] The /n/ before /na/ is the 3rd person pronoun, referencing the god as the person for whom the temple was built.

Lesson Five

1. lugal-e e₂ mu-un-du₃

/lugal.e e₂.ø mu.n.du₃/

"The king built the house"

The word /lugal/ has the ergative marker /e/, making it

---

[59] Case elements are not always written in cuneiform texts (as they are here), but we will often put them into our transliterations so that others can see how we understand the grammar of a sentence!

the agent of the transitive verb /du₃/, which is in the *ḫamtu* or "past" tense. The /n/ before the verbal base /du₃/ refers to the 3rd person animate agent /lugal/. The /e₂/ is the object of the transitive verb.

2. diĝir-re ĝeštug₂ mu-un-šum₂

/diĝir.e ĝeštug₂.ø mu.n.šum₂/

"The god listened"

The noun /diĝir/ has the ergative marker /e/, and is the agent of the compound verb /ĝeštug₂—šum₂/ "to give ear; listen." The /n/ before the verbal base /šum₂/ marks the *ḫamtu* 3rd person animate agent /diĝir/, marked with the ergative /e/.

3. lu₂-e alan mu-dim₂-e

/lu₂.e alan.ø mu.dim₂.e/

"The man will fashion the statue"

The noun /lu₂/ is marked with the ergative /e/, making it the agent of the transitive verb /dim₂/ "to form, fashion." Because an /e/ follows the transitive verb /dim₂/, it is marking it as a *marû* or "present/future" tense verb, and it refers to the 3rd person animate agent /lu₂/ in the sentence.

4. nin uru-še₃ ba-gi₄

/nin.ø uru.še₃ ba.gi₄/

"The lady returned to the city"

The noun /nin/ is the subject of the intransitive verb /gi₄/ "to return," and the noun /uru/ "city" is marked with the preposition /-še₃/ "to, toward." We know that the verb /gi₄/ is *ḫamtu*, since the *marû* form of /gi₄/ is reduplicated /gi₄-gi₄/.

5. en e₂-še₃ ba-gi₄-gi₄

   /en.ø e₂.še₃ ba.gi₄.gi₄/

   "The lord will return to the house"

   This is the same construction as seen in example 4, but the verbal base /gi₄/ is reduplicated /gi₄-gi₄/, which makes it a *marû* verb.

6. dig̃ir lugal-ra mu-na-du₁₁

   /dig̃ir.e lugal.ra mu.na.n.du₁₁/

   "The god spoke to the king"

   The verb /du₁₁/ is the *ḫamtu* form of the verb. Although the ergative /e/ does not appear on /dig̃ir/, and the /n/ before the verbal base /du₁₁/ is not written, I have written them in the normalization. The /-ra/ on /lugal/ is the dative.

7. nin dig̃ir-ra mu-na-e

   /nin.e dig̃ir.ra mu.na.e/

   "The lady will speak to the god"

This is the same construction as in example 6; however, /e/ is the *marû* form of /du$_{11}$/, making it the present/future tense.

8. ama-e a mu-tum$_2$

   /ama.e a.ø mu.tum$_2$/

   "The mother will bring water"

   The noun /ama/ is in the ergative case /e/, and /tum$_2$/ is the *marû* form of the verb /de$_6$/ "to carry, bring." The noun /a/ "water" is marked with a /ø/, as it is the object of the verb /tum$_2$/.

9. lugal-e niĝ$_2$ mu-de$_6$-de$_6$

   /lugal.e niĝ$_2$.ø mu.n.de$_6$.de$_6$/

   "The king brought things."

   The noun /lugal/ is marked with the ergative /e/. The verb /de$_6$/ is the *ḫamtu* form of the verb, but it is reduplicated. This is a case of *ḫamtu* reduplication, which likely refers to the plurality of the object in the sentence, which is /niĝ$_2$/ "thing."

10. mu-gi$_4$-gi$_4$

   /mu.gi$_4$.gi$_4$/

   "He will return"

   The verb is the reduplicated *marû* form of /gi$_4$/ "to return".

11. mu-bad-e

/mu.bad.e/

"He will open"

The verb is /bad/ "to open", marked as a *marû* form by the /-e/.

Lesson Six

1. e₂-g̃u₁₀

/e₂.g̃u₁₀/

"my house"

lugal-zu

/lugal.zu/

"your king"

ama-ni

/ama.ani/

"his mother"

2. bad₃-bi

/bad₃.bi/

"its wall"

nin-a-ni

/nin.ani/

"his lady"

lu$_2$-ĝu$_{10}$-ne-ra

/lu$_2$.ĝu$_{10}$.ene.ra/

"to my men"

3. ĝa$_2$-e e$_2$-a i$_3$-ĝen-ne-en

/ĝa$_2$.e e$_2$.a i$_3$.ĝen.en/

"I walked into the house"

The form /ĝa$_2$-e/ is the 1st person singular personal pronoun ("I"), and is the subject of the intransitive verb /ĝen/ "to go". The ending /-ne-en/ represents the duplicated /n/ from /ĝen/ to connect the intransitive 1st person singular ending /-en/ to the verb. Finally, the /-a/ on /e$_2$-a/ is the locative.

4. lugal-e za-ra mu-un-du$_{11}$

/lugal.e za.ra mu.n.du$_{11}$/

"The king spoke to you"

The /e/ on /lugal/ is the ergative, making it the agent of the verb /du$_{11}$/. The /n/ before /du$_{11}$/ references the 3rd person animate agent /lugal-e/. The form /za-ra/ is the 2nd person pronoun with the dative suffix.

5. i$_3$-re$_7$-en-de$_3$-en

/i$_3$.re$_7$.enden/

"we went"

The form /re₇/ is the *ḫamtu* plural of the verb /ĝen/, and the ending /enden/ is the 1st person plural intransitive marker.

6. e-ne-ne eden-ta i₃-re₇-eš

   /e.ne.ne eden.ta i₃.re₇.eš/

   "They walked (away) from the steppe"

   The form /e.ne.ne/ is the 3rd person plural pronoun "they," which is represented in the verb by the ending /-eš/. The /-ta/ on /eden/ is the ablative "from."

7. e-ne e₂-a i₃-ku₄

   /e.ne e₂.a i₃.ku₄.ø/

   "He entered into the house"

   The form /e.ne/ is the 3rd person singular pronoun. The /a/ on /e₂/ is the locative "in."

8. eden-ta uru-še₃ i₃-re₇-en-ze₂-en

   /eden.ta uru.še₃ i₃.re₇.enzen/

   "You went from the steppe to the city"

   The verbal ending /-enzen/ is the 2nd person plural ("you"). The ablative /-ta/ "from" shows motion away from the steppe, while the terminative /-še₃/ "to" shows motion toward the city.

9. lu₂ ᵍⁱˢeren-da uru-a i₃-g̃en

   /lu₂.ø ᵍⁱˢeren.da uru.a i₃.g̃en/

   "The man went into the city with cedar wood"

   The /lu₂/ is the subject of the intransitive verb /g̃en/.

   The /a/ on /uru/ is the locative "in", while the /-da/ on

   /ᵍⁱˢeren/ is the comitative "with."

10. dumu-a-ni

    /dumu.ani/

    "His son"

11. e₂-zu

    /e₂.zu/

    "Your house"

12. dig̃ir-ra lugal-e ma₂ mu-na-dim₂-e

    /dig̃ir.ra lugal.e ma₂.ø mu.na.dim₂.e

    "The king will fashion the boat for the god"

    /dig̃ir/ is marked in the dative case /-ra/, which is

    complemented by the /-na-/ in the verbal chain. The

    verb is in the *marû*, with the agent /lugal/ marked

    with the ergative /-e/ and the 3ʳᵈ person /-e/.

13. munus-e mu-un-dim₂

    /munus.e mu.n.dim₂.ø/

    "The woman fashioned"

The agent is marked with an /-e/, and the /-n-/ in the verbal chain is the *ḫamtu* 3rd person agent marker.

Lesson Seven

1. lu₂-e e₂-a še mu-un-g̃ar

   /lu₂.e e₂.a še.ø mu.n.g̃ar.ø/

   "The man set grain in the house"

   The /e/ on /lu₂/ is the ergative, cross-referenced in the verbal chain by the /n/ before /g̃ar/, showing it to be a *ḫamtu* 3rd person singular verb. /še/ is the direct object, marked with a /ø/, and the /a/ on /e₂/ is the locative "in."

2. lugal-le-ne i₃ mu-un-de₂-eš

   /lugal.ene i₃.ø mu.n.de₂.eš/

   "The kings poured out oil"

   The verb /de₂/ is preceded by an /n/ and followed by an /eš/, which marks the 3rd person plural agent of a *ḫamtu* verb. This cross-references the plural noun /lugal.ene/ "kings." Finally, the /i₃/ is the direct object of the verb /de₂/ "to pour out."

3. gu₃-de₂-a kaš bi₂-in-nag̃

   /gu₃.de₂.a.e kaš.ø bi₂.n.nag̃.ø/

"Gudea drank beer"

The personal name "Gudea" is the agent of the transitive verb /nağ/ "to drink." We know that it is in the ḫamtu for two reasons: first, if it were in the marû, it would be reduplicated (/naₛ-naₛ/). Second, it is preceded by an /n/, which often marks the 3rd person singular agent. Finally, /kaš/ is the direct object.

4. piriḡ eden-ta ba-ta-ḡen

   /piriḡ.ø eden.ta ba.ta.ḡen/

   "The lion went out from the steppe"

   Because /ḡen/ is an intransitive verb, /piriḡ/ is marked with a /ø/ as its subject. The /-ta-/ in the verbal chain is cross-referenced by the /-ta/ on /eden/.

5. piriḡ-e udu mu-ub-gu₇

   /piriḡ.e udu.ø mu.b.gu₇.ø/

   "The lion ate the sheep"

   The noun /piriḡ/ is marked with the ergative, and is the subject of the ḫamtu verb /gu₇/, which is marked with a /b/ before the verbal base. /udu/ is the direct object, marked with a /ø/.

6. ᵈutu-ra an-še₃ šu ba-e-zig₃-ge-en-ze₂-en

   /ᵈutu.ra an.še₃ šu.ø ba.e.zig₃.enzen/

   "You raised (your) hand toward heaven to Utu"

The verb /šu—zig$_3$/ "to raise the hand" is marked as a *hamtu* 2nd person plural by the /e/ before the verbal base /zig$_3$/ and the /enzen/ after. The phrase /an-še$_3$/ means "to heaven," and the dative /-ra/ is attached to the divine name /^{d}utu/.

7. lugal-e e$_2$ mu-un-bad

   /lugal.e e$_2$.ø mu.n.bad.ø/

   "The king opened the temple"

   This is a *hamtu* transitive verb, with the agent marked with an /-e/ ergative marker, and an /-n-/ 3rd person animate marker in the verbal chain. The direct object is marked with /-ø/.

8. e$_2$ mu-du$_3$-en-de$_3$-en

   /e$_2$.ø mu.ø.du$_3$.enden/

   "We built the temple"

   This is a *hamtu* transitive verb, with the agent marked in the verbal chain with the 1st person plural animate marker. Note that there is no object marker in the verbal chain in this instance, although the noun /e$_2$/ that functions as the direct object is still normalized with the /-ø/ marker.

Lesson Eight

1. e₂ mu-ub-du₃-en

   /e₂.ø mu.b.du₃.en/

   "I/You will build the house"

   The verb /du₃/ has a /b/ before the verbal base, and an
   /-en/ after it. The verbal form should be understood as
   a *marû* 1ˢᵗ or 2ⁿᵈ singular transitive verb (/-en/), with a
   3ʳᵈ inanimate singular object (/b/). In that case, we
   would translate, "I/You will build it…" Since there is
   an inanimate noun in the sentence /e₂/, we would
   understand that to be the inanimate object.

2. kaskal-la g̃eštin mu-de₂-en-de₃-en

   /kaskal.a g̃eštin.ø mu.de₂.enden/

   "We will pour out wine in the road"

   The ending /-enden/ likely tells us that this is either an
   intransitive verb (either *ḫamtu* or *marû*) or a *marû*
   transitive verb (1ˢᵗ person plural). The noun /g̃eštin/
   "wine" has no marking, so it is likely the direct object
   of the verb /de₂/ "to pour out." Finally, /kaskal/ has an
   /a/, which is likely the locative "in."

3. ᵈinanna šu-ni-še₃ me mu-la₂-e

   /ᵈinanna.e šu.ani.še₃ me.ø mu.la₂.e/

   "Inanna hangs the Mes on her hand"

The /e/ at the end of the verbal form is *marû* 3rd singular transitive marker, which corresponds to the agent in the sentence /ᵈinanna/. The noun /me/ is the direct object of the verb. Finally, the phrase /šu.ani.še₃/ has the terminative "to" attached to "her hand."

4. lugal-e kur-ra mu-ni mu-g̃a₂-g̃a₂

   /lugal.e kur.a mu.ani.ø mu.g̃a₂.g̃a₂/

   "The king will set his name in the mountain"

   We can see that the verb /g̃a₂-g̃a₂/ is a transitive *marû* verb, as we learned that this is the *marû* form of the verb /g̃ar/. The ergative /e/ can be seen on /lugal/, making it the agent. This leaves the forms /kur-ra mu-ni/. The /a/ on /kur/ is the locative "in," and /mu.ani/ is written only with the /-ni/, as /mu/ ends in a vowel.

5. lu₂-e e₂ dig̃ir-ra-ke₄ ki mu-us₂-e

   /lu₂.e e₂ dig̃ir.ak.e ki.ø mu.us₂.e/

   "The man will establish the house of the god"

   The compound verb /ki—us₂/ is *marû*, as the /us₂/ portion of the verb is followed by an /e/ with the noun /ki/ is its object (/ø/). The agent is clear (/lu₂-e/). This leaves /e₂ dig̃ir-ra-ke₄/. The first thing that catches our eye is the /k/ at the end of /dig̃ir-ra-ke₄/; this should tell us that we are probably looking at a genitive construction. This leaves the /e/ on /e₂ dig̃ir.ak.e/. We remember that, when we have a compound verb, it often marks its direct object (since the noun part of the compound verb is already a direct object) with the locative-terminative or the locative (and even, sometimes, with no marking at all). Here, we have a locative-terminative /e/.

6. lugal-e e₂ mu-ub-du₃-e

/lugal.c e₂.ø mu.b.du₃.e/

"The king will build the temple"

This is a transitive *marû* verbal form, with the 3rd person animate agent marker /-e/ placed after the verb in the verbal chain, with the /-e/ ergative marker on /lugal/. The direct object is marked with the inanimate /-b-/ before the verbal base, and /e₂/ is marked with /ø/ as the direct object of a transitive verb.

7. diĝir-e alan i₃-ib-dim₂-e

/diĝir.e alan.ø i₃.b.dim₂.e/

"The god will fashion the statue"

This sentence is grammatically identical to number six!

Lesson Nine

1. lugal e₂-kur-še₃ nu-ĝen

/lugal.ø e₂.kur.še₃ nu.ĝen.ø/

"The king did not go to the Ekur"

Beginning with the verb, the /nu/ is the "negative," changing the verb from "he went" to "he did *not* go." The noun /lugal/ is the subject, marked with a /ø/, and the terminative /še₃/ shows the king going "toward" the Ekur (the name of a temple).

2. e-ne ᵍⁱpisag̃ he₂-tum₃

   /e.ne ᵍⁱpisag̃.ø he₂.tum₃/

   "Let him bring a reed basket"

   We should begin by translating the modal prefix /he₂/ "let him..." The verb /tum₃/ is the *marû* form of the verb /de₆/, and the personal pronoun /e.ne/ is its agent. Finally, the noun /ᵍⁱpisag̃/ is the direct object, marked with a /ø/.

3. dig̃ir lugal-še₃ me-lim₄-a-ni mu-un-šum₂

   /dig̃ir.e lugal.še₃ me.lim₄.ani.ø mu.n.šum₂.ø/

   "The god gave his frightening splendor to the king"

   The verb /šum₂/ is in the *hamtu*, marked by the /n/ before the verbal base. I have written the ergative /e/ on /dig̃ir/, though it does not appear in the writing. Because a /še₃/ appears on /lugal/, we translate it "to the king," which leaves /me-lim₄-a-ni/ as the direct object.

4. ^{d}en-ki lugal abzu-ke$_4$ ba-an-du$_{11}$

   /^{d}en.ki lugal abzu.ak.e ba.n.du$_{11}$.ø/

   "Enki, king of the Abzu, spoke"

   In this sentence, /^{d}en-ki/ stands in apposition[60] to /lugal abzu-ke$_4$/. In other words, both "Enki" and "king of the Abzu" are the same being. Notice that there is only one ergative /e/ that appears on the second appositional phrase. Sumerian allows for a grammatical marker like the ergative to be put on the end of several appositional nouns or phrases, but mark all of them. The form /abzu-ke$_4$/ contains the genitive /ak/, written only with the /k/, as it follows a vowel and is followed by another marker. Finally, I have identified the /an/ in the verbal chain as the *ḫamtu* 3rd singular marker, but it could just as easily be the 3rd person dative /na/.

5. ^{d}en-lil$_2$-ra šu ga-na-mu$_2$

   /^{d}en.lil$_2$.ra šu.ø ga.na.mu$_2$/

   "Let me pray to Enlil"

   The prefix /ga/ on the verb tells us that this is a cohortative, and because we have no /enden/ ending, it is a 1st singular. The /na/ in the verbal chain is the

---

[60] "Apposition" just means that "Enki" and "king of the Abzu" are next to each other and refer to the same thing.

dative, cross-referenced in the sentence with the /-ra/ on Enlil. Finally, the verb is a compound (/šu—mu₂/); thus, /šu/ is marked with a /ø/ as the direct object.

6. ga-mu-du₃

/ga.mu.du₃/

"Let me build"

This is a cohortative 3ʳᵈ animate singular construction.

7. lugal-e e₂ nu-mu-un-bad

/lugal.e e₂.ø nu.mu.n.bad.ø/

"The king did not open the temple"

This is a negative *ḫamtu* transitive verb (marked with /nu-/), with /lugal/ as the agent, marked with the ergative /-e/, and /-n/ in the verbal chain. The temple is the direct object, marked with /-ø/ on both the noun and verbal chain.

8. ḫe₂-mu-tuš-e

/ḫe₂.mu.tuš.e/

"Let him sit"

This is a precative verbal construction (/ḫe₂/), with the agent marked in the verbal chain with the 3ʳᵈ person singular animate marker /-e/.

Lesson Ten

1. ur-saĝ ša₃ nu-ḫul₂

   /ur.saĝ.e ša₃.ø nu.n.ḫul₂.ø/

   "The hero was not happy"

   The compound verb /ša₃—ḫul₂/ is negated with /nu/, with /ur.saĝ/ as the agent.

2. gu₃-de₂-a maš₂-a šu i₃-gid₂ maš₂-a-ni i₃-sag₉

   /gu₃.de₂.a.e maš₂.a šu.ø i₃.n.gid₂.ø maš₂.ani.ø i₃.sag₉.ø/

   "Gudea performed extispicy on the goat; his omen was good"

   The first verbal form consists of the compound verb /šu—gid₂/ "to perform extispicy," with Gudea as the agent. The noun /maš₂/ is marked with the locative, which shows it to be the "oblique object" of the compound verb. In the second part of the line has the verb /sag₉/ with the subject /maš₂.ani.ø/.

3. lugal-e siskur₂-ra-na šu ba-an-ti

   /lugal.e siskur₂.ani.a šu.ø ba.n.ti.ø/

   "The king accepted his sacrifice"

   The noun /lugal/ is in the ergative and is the agent of the compound verb /šu—ti/, which is a *ḫamtu* 3rd person singular, marked by the /n/ before the verbal base. The form /siskur₂-ra-na/ contains an /r/ auslaut, the suffix /.ani/, and the locative /a/, which marks the oblique object of the compound verb.

4. nin-e nam-maḫ-a-ni pa e₃ bi₂-in-ak
/nin.e nam.maḫ.ani.e pa.ø e₃ bi₂.n.ak.ø/
"The lady made manifest her magnificence"
The compound verb /pa—e₃/ is constructed with an "auxiliary verb" /ak/, with /nin/ as its agent. The /ni/ sign can also be read /ne₂/, which represents /.ani/ + /e/ (locative-terminative), which marks the oblique object of the compound verb.

5. nin-e e₂-e ki mu-un-ãg₂
/nin.e e₂.e ki.ø mu.n.ãg₂.ø
"The lady loved the temple"
This is a compound verb, /ki—ãg₂/, with the noun /nin/ marked with the ergative as the agent, corresponding to the /-n-/ in the verbal chain. The oblique object of the compound verb (/e₂/) is marked with the locative-terminative case marker /-e/.

6. kur maḫ-še₃ lugal-e igi mu-ub-ši-ãar
/kur maḫ.še₃ lugal.e igi.ø mu.b.ši.n.ãar.ø/
"The king looked toward the majestic land"
The compound verb is /igi—ãar/, and the agent is /lugal/, marked with the ergative /-e/. The terminative

case ending /še$_3$/ is attached to the phrase /kur maḫ/, indicating the direction in which the king is looking.

Lesson Eleven

1. lugal-ra du$_{11}$-ga-ab

   /lugal.ra du$_{11}$.i$_3$.b/

   "Say it to the king!"

   The imperative form of /du$_{11}$/ shows the expected /g/ of the auslaut for /du$_{11}$/, followed by an /a/ vowel (representing /i$_3$/), and a /b/ for the 3rd inanimate object. The /ra/ on /lugal/ is the dative.

2. nin-ra maš$_2$ šum$_2$-mu-na-ab

   /nin.ra maš$_2$.ø šum$_2$.i$_3$.na.b/

   "Give the goat to the lady!"

   The imperative of /šum$_2$/ contains a /na/ in the verbal chain, as well as a /b/ for the object (/maš$_2$/). The dative /ra/ appears on the noun /nin/.

3. ^{d}en-ki en nam tar-tar-re-de$_3$

   /^{d}en.ki en nam tar.tar.ede/

   "Enki, the lord who determines fates"

   The compound verb /nam—tar/ is marked as a *marû* participle with /.ede/. We began by translating it as "the one who..." The noun "Enki" stands in apposition to the rest of the line.

4. e₂ du₃-de₃ e₂ ki us₂-se-de₃

   /e₂.ø du₃.ede e₂.ø ki.ø us₂.ede/

   "in order to build the house, in order to firmly ground the house"

   Both verbs appear as *marû* participles, marked with /.ede/. We could also translate these, "The one who…, the one who…" Only context will determine the appropriate interpretation.

5. lugal lu₂ e₂-še₃ ba-g̃en-a i₃-gub

   /lugal lu₂ e₂.še₃ ba.g̃en.ø.a.ø i₃.gub.ø/

   "The king, who went to the temple, stood."

   The use of /lu₂/ and /a/ mark the phrase "went to the temple" as a subordinate clause.

6. du₃-ma-ab

   du₃.mu.b

   "Build it!"

   This is an imperative construction, with the /b/ representing the 3ʳᵈ inanimate object.

7. la₂-ma-ab

   la₂.mu.b

   "Hang it!"

   Another imperative!

8. lugal-e diĝir ki aĝ₂-ĝa₂-de₃

lugal.e diĝir.ø ki.ø aĝ₂.ede

"The king who loves the god"

This is a *marû* participle, with /lugal/ marked in the ergative as the agent, and then again in the verbal chain with the /ede/ 3rd animate singular marker.

Royal Inscriptions

Inscription 1

1. ᵈba.u₂

2. munus sag₉.a

3. dumu an.ak

4. nin uru ku₃.a.ak

5. nin.ani.ra

6. gu₃.de₂.a

7. ensi₂

8. lagaš^ki.ak.e

9. e₂ uru ku₃.a.ak.ani.ø

10. mu.na.n.du₃.ø

"For Bau, the beautiful woman, child of An, the lady of the holy city, his lady, Gudea, the ruler of Lagaš, built her house of the holy city."

The divine name /ᵈba-u₂/ is in apposition to all of the epithets found in lines 2-5, which are all in the dative case (although the /-ra/ is not written in the text). We know that it is in the dative, as there is a /na/ in the verbal chain. The noun /munus/ is modified by the adjective /sag$_9$.a/. The nouns /dumu/ and /an/ are in a genitive construction. The noun /nin/ is in a genitive construction with /uru/, which is modified by the adjective /ku$_3$/. Gudea is in apposition to the genitive phrase "king of Lagaš," and both are marked with a single ergative /e/. The object of the verb /du$_3$/, which is in the *ḫamtu* 3rd person singular, is the phrase /e$_2$ uru ku$_3$.a.ak.ani.ø/. The /ø/ marks the entire phrase as the object, along with the possessive suffix /ani/. As in line 4, the noun /e$_2$/ is in a genitive construction with /uru/, which is modified by /ku$_3$.a/.

Inscription 2

1. ^{d}en.lil$_2$
2. lugal diĝir.ene.ak.ra
3. eš$_3$ nibru^{ki}.ak
4. dur.an.ki.še$_3$
5. gu$_3$.de$_2$.a
6. ensi$_2$
7. lagaš^{ki}.ak
8. ma$_2$.gid$_2$
9. e$_2$.kur.ak.e

10. nam.til.ani.še₃

11. a.ø mu.na.ru

"For Enlil, king of the gods, for the shine of Nippur, Duranki, Gudea, the ruler of Lagash, the boat-tower of the Ekur, dedicated (this object) for the sake of his life."

The divine name Enlil has one appositional phrase, "king of the gods"; the /-ra/ dative (marked with the /-na-/ in the verbal chain) marks both phrases. The /-še₃/ in line 4 is interesting; it probably carries the idea of "(destined) for" or "for (the sake of)." The name Gudea, along with the phrase "boat-tower of the Ekur", are marked with the ergative /-e/ in line 9. The /-še₃/ in line 10 is a common use "for the sake of," with the compound verb /a—ru/ "to dedicate."

Inscription 3

1. ᵈinanna

2. nin kur.kur.ak

3. nin.ani.ra

4. gu₃.de₂.a

5. ensi₂

6. lagašᵏⁱ.ak

7. ur ᵈg̃a₂.tum₃.du₁₀.ak.e

8. e₂.an.na g̃ir₂.suᵏⁱ.ak.ani.ø

9. mu.na.n.du₃.ø

"For Inanna, the lady of all the lands, his lady, Gudea, the ruler of Lagaš, the man of Gatumdu, built her Eanna of Girsu."

The divine name /ᵈinanna/ is in apposition to "lady of all the lands," as well as "his lady." We have added the dative /ra/ to /nin-a-ni/. Gudea is the agent of the verb, with the ergative /e/ coming after the epithets "ruler of Lagaš" and "man of Gatumdu." Finally, the object that Gudea built was "her Eanna of Girsu."

Inscription 4

1. ᵈinanna
2. nin kur.kur.ak
3. nin.ani.ra
4. gu₃.de₂.a
5. ensi₂
6. lagaš^{ki}.ak.e
7. e₂.an.na g̃ir₂.su^{ki}.ak.ani.ø
8. mu.na.n.du₃.ø

"For Inanna, lady of all the lands, his lady, Gudea, ruler of Lagaš, built her Eanna of Girsu."

This inscription is exactly like Inscription 3, except that the epithet "man of Gatumdu" is not present. This results in the /-ke₄/ moving up one line, attaching itself to /lagaš^{ki}/.

Inscription 5

1. ^{d}nin.a.zu

2. diĝir.ani.ra

3. gu₃.de₂.a

4. ensi₂

5. lagaš^{ki}.ak.e

6. e₂ ĝir₂.su^{ki}.ak.ani.ø

7. mu.na.n.du₃.ø

"For Ninazu, his god, Gudea, the ruler of Lagaš, build his house of Girsu."

The divine name "Ninazu" is in apposition to "his god," which we have marked with the dative /-ra/. Gudea, the agent, stands in apposition to "ruler of Lagaš," which is marked with the ergative /e/. Finally, the object of the verb is "his house of Girsu."

Inscription 6

1. ^{d}nin.ĝir₂.su

2. ur.saĝ kala.a

3. ^{d}en.lil₂.ak.ra

4. gu₃.de₂.a

5. ensi₂

6. lagaš^{ki}.ak.e

7. niĝ₂.du₇.e pa.ø mu.na.n.e₃.ø

8. e$_2$.ninnu anzu$_2^{mušen}$ babbar$_2$.a.ani.ø

9. mu.na.n.du$_3$.ø

"For Ningirsu, the mighty hero of Enlil, Gudea, the ruler of Lagaš, made manifest appropriate things; he built his Eninnu, the shining Anzu bird."

The divine name /^{d}nin.g̃ir$_2$.su/ is in apposition to the epithet "mighty hero of Enlil," all of which is marked with the dative /-ra/. Gudea is the agent of both verbs, and is in apposition to "ruler of Lagaš" (as in the other inscriptions). The first verb, /pa—e$_3$/, marks its oblique object (/nig̃$_2$.du$_7$/) with the locative-terminative /e/. The second verb marks its direct object /e$_2$.ninnu anzu$_2^{mušen}$ babbar.a.ani/ with a /ø/. The phrase "shining Anzu bird" stands in apposition to "Eninnu."

Inscription 7

1. ^{d}nin.g̃ir$_2$.su

2. ur.sag̃ kala.a

3. ^{d}en.lil$_2$.ak

4. lugal.ani.ra

5. gu$_3$.de$_2$.a

6. ensi$_2$

7. lagaš^{ki}.ak.e

8. e$_2$ ba.gara$_2$.ak.ani.ø

9. mu.na.n.du$_3$.ø

The divine name "Ningirsu" is again in apposition to "mighty hero of Enlil" and "his king," which we have marked with the dative /-ra/. Gudea is again the agent, along with the epithet "ruler of Lagaš," marked by the ergative /e/. The object of the verb /du₃/ is "his house of Bagara."

Inscription 8

1. ᵈnin.sumun₂
2. diĝir.ani.ra
3. ur.ᵈnammu
4. nita kala.a
5. lugal uri₅ᵏⁱ.ak
6. lugal ki.en.gi ki.uri.ak.e
7. e₂.maḫ
8. e₂ ki.ø aĝ₂.a.ani.ø
9. mu.na.n.du₃.ø

"For Ninsumun, his god, Ur-Nammu, the mighty man, the king of Ur, the king of Sumer and Akkad, build the Emaḫ, his beloved house."

The divine name "Ninsumun" is in apposition to "his god," which we have marked with a dative /-ra/. Ur-Nammu is the agent, marked with an ergative /e/ after the following epithets. Notice that /lugal ki.en.gi ki.uri/ only requires one genitive marker, rather than a genitive after /ki.en.gi/ and

/ki.uri/. Finally, the object of the verb /du₃/ is /e₂.maḫ/, which has an appositional phrase "his beloved house." Notice that the compound verb /ki—aĝ₂/, marked with an /a/ to show the participle, is acting as a modifier of /e₂/, and the entire phrase is marked with the possessive suffix /.ani/ "his."

Inscription 9

1. ur.ᵈnammu

2. lugal uri₅ᵏⁱ.ak

3. lugal ki.en.gi ki.uri.ak

4. lu₂ e₂ ᵈen.lil₂.ak.e

5. i₃.n.du₃.ø.a

"Ur-Nammu, the king of Ur, the king of Sumer and Akkad, the one who built the house of Enlil"

The agent of the verb appears first, as no deity is mentioned in the dative case. As in the other inscriptions, there are several appositional phrases that function as epithets for Ur-Nammu. In line 4, the /lu₂/ connects to the /a/ at the end of the inscription makes the verb and its agent (/lu₂/) part of a dependent clause – "The one who…"

Inscription 10

1. ᵈen.lil₂

2. lugal kur.kur.ak

3. lugal.ani.ra

4. ur.^{d}nammu

5. nita kala.a

6. lugal uri$_5$^{ki}.ak

7. lugal ki.en.gi ki.uri.ak.e

8. e$_2$.kur

9. e$_2$ ki.ø ag̃$_2$.a.ani.ø

10. mu.na.n.du$_3$.ø

"For Enlil, the king of all the lands, his king, Ur-Nammu, the mighty man, the king of Ur, the king of Sumer and Akkad, built the Ekur, his beloved house."

This inscription follows the same pattern as those that we have seen. Enlil and his epithets are in the dative case, while Ur-Nammu and his epithets are in the ergative. The Ekur, with its epithet "his beloved house" stands as the direct object of the verb /du$_3$/.

Inscription 11

1. ^{d}inanna

2. nin.ani.ra

3. ^{d}bur.^{d}en.zu

4. lugal kala.a

5. lugal ki.en.gi ki.uri.ak.e

6. mu.na.n.dim$_2$.ø

7. nam.ti.ani.še₃

8. a.ø mu.na.n.ru.ø

"For Inanna, his lady, Bur-Suen, the mighty king, the king of Sumer and Akkad, fashioned (this object). For the sake of his life he dedicated (it)."

Inanna and her epithet are marked in the dative case, shown with the form /ir/ on /ani/ in line 2. The king Bur-Suen is the agent of both verbs, though neither the genitive nor the ergative appear on /ki-uri/, as it ends in a vowel. The dative /na/ in both verbal chains references the /ra/ on /nin.ani.ra/, and the compound verb /a—ru/ "to dedicate" has an unspecified object (the object on which the inscription appears), which is dedicated "for the sake of" (/še₃/) his life.

Inscription 12

1. ᵈbur.ᵈsuen

2. lugal kala.a

3. lugal ki.en.gi ki.uri.ak

4. ab.ba.mu

5. dub.sar

6. dumu lu₂.ᵈutu.ak

7. ir₃.zu

"Bur-Suen, the mighty king, king of Sumer and Akkad: your servant, Abba-mu, the scribe, son of Lu-Utu."

This is a seal inscription of a servant of the king Bur-Suen
(/en-zu/ is normalized /suen/). The grammar is relatively
straightforward, as there are no verbal forms associated with
it. The seal simply identifies who the owner is.

Year Names

Šulgi

1. mu šul.gi lugal
"Year: Šulgi *became* king"

2. mu g̃iri₃ nibru^ki.ak.ø si.ø bi₂.n.sa₂.ø
"Year: he set the road of Nippur straight"

3. mu e₂.ḫur.sag̃ lugal.ak.ø ba.du₃
"Year: the Eḫursag̃ (temple) of the king was built"

4. mu ^g̃iš na₂ ^d nin.lil₂.ak.ø ba.dim₂
"Year: the bed of Ninlil was fashioned"

5. mu bad₃.an^ki ba.ḫul
"Year: (The city of) Der was destroyed"

6. mu us₂.a bad₃.an^ki ba.ḫul
"Year: The year after the year (the city of) Der was
destroyed"

7. mu ᵈšul.gi lugal.e bad₃ ma.da.ak.ø mu.n.du₃.ø

"Year: Šulgi the king built the wall of the land"

Translations from Cuneiform

Hand Copy 1, P226644

1. ᵈnanna	ᵈnanna
2. lugal-a-ni	lugal.ani.ra
3. ur-ᵈnammu	ur.ᵈnammu
4. lugal uri₅ᵏⁱ-ma-ke₄	lugal uri₅ᵏⁱ.ak.e
5. e₂-a-ni	e₂.ani.ø
6. mu-na-du₃	mu.na.n.du₃.ø
7. bad₃ uri₅ᵏⁱ-ma	bad₃ uri₅ᵏⁱ.ak.ø
8. mu-na-du₃	mu.na.n.du₃.ø

"For Nanna, his king, Ur-Nammu, king of Ur, built his temple (and) built the wall of Ur."

As with previous inscriptions, Nanna is in the dative case, as shown by the /-na-/ in both verbal chains. Ur-Nammu is the agent of the sentence, shown by the ergative /-e/. The temple in line 5 is marked with the possessive suffix /-ani/, indicating its relationship to Nanna, and is the direct object of the verb in line 6. The "wall" is marked with the genitive /-ak/ to indicate that it is the wall *of* Ur. It is the direct object of the final verb in line 8.

Hand Copy 2, P. 226818

1. ur-^{d}nammu ur.^{d}nammu

2. lugal uri$_5^{ki}$-ma lugal uri$_5^{ki}$.ak

3. lu$_2$ e$_2$ ^{d}nin-sun$_2$ lu$_2$ e$_2$ ^{d}nin.sun.ak

4. in-du$_3$-a i$_3$.n.du$_3$.ø.a

"Ur-Nammu, king of Ur, the one who built the temple of Ninsun."

This inscription also contains the subordinate construction. The /lu$_2$/ connects with the /-a/ in line 4 and is translated, "The one who..."

Hand Copy 3, P232332

1. ^{d}ba-u$_2$ ^{d}ba.u$_2$

2. munus sag$_9$-ga munus sag$_9$.a

3. dumu an-na dumu an.ak

4. nin uru ku$_3$-ga nin uru ku$_3$.a.ak

5. nin-a-ni nin.ani.ra

6. gu$_3$-de$_2$-a gu$_3$.de$_2$.a

7. ensi$_2$ ensi$_2$

8. lagaš^{ki} lagaš^{ki}.ak

9. lu$_2$ e$_2$-ninnu lu$_2$ e$_2$.ninnu

10. ^{d}nin-gir$_2$-su-ka ^{d}nin.gir$_2$.su.ak

11. e$_2$-PA e$_2$ ub imin-a-ni e$_2$.PA e$_2$ ub imin.ani.ø

12. mu-du$_3$-a mu.n.du$_3$.ø.a

13. e₂ uru ku₃-ga-ka-ni   e₂ uru ku₃.a.ak.ani.ø

14. mu-na-du₃   mu.na.n.du₃.ø

"For Bau, the good woman, daughter of An, lady of the pure city, his lady, Gudea, ruler of Lagash, the one who built the Eninnu of Ningirsu, the ... house, the seven-cornered house, built her temple of the pure city."

As in other inscriptions, the dative /-ra/ is not specifically marked in line 5, but the infix /-na-/ in line 13 lets us know that it is implied. Again we see the subordinate construction, with the /lu₂/ in line 9 and the /-a/ following the verb in line 11. It is unclear what /PA/ means in line 11.

Hand Copy 4, P226202

1. ᵈnimin-tab-ba   ᵈnimin.tab.ba

2. nin-a-ni   nin.ani.ra

3. šul-gi   šul.gi

4. nita kala-ga   nita kala.a

5. lugal uri₅ᵏⁱ-ma   lugal uri₅ᵏⁱ.ak

6. lugal ki-en-gi   lugal ki.en.gi

    ki-uri-ke₄   ki.uri.ak.e

7. e₂-a-ni   e₂.ani.ø

8. mu-na-du₃   mu.na.n.du₃.ø

"For Nimintabba, his lady, Šulgi, mighty man, king of Ur, king of Sumer and Akkad, built her temple."

Appendix B

Appendix C

Glossary of Sumerian Words

a	water
a$_2$	arm, power
a$_2$—ag̃$_2$	to command
a—ru	to dedicate
a-a	father
abzu	Abzu
an	An, heaven, sky
a-nun-na	Anuna gods
ak	to do, make
alan	statue
alim	bison
ama	mother
amar	calf
an-ub-da	corner
anzu^{mušen}	Anzu bird
anzu$_2$^{mušen}	Anzu bird
babbar	white
babbar$_2$	white, to shine
bad	to open, be remote
bad$_3$	wall
bad$_3$-an^{ki}	Der

ba-gara$_2$	Bagara
^{d}ba-u$_2$	Bau
bur-^{d}en-zu	Bur-Suen
dab$_5$	to seize
dam	spouse
de$_2$	to pour out
de$_6$	to bring, carry
diĝir	god
dim$_2$	to form, fashion
du$_3$	to build
du$_{10}$	to be good
du$_{11}$	to say, speak
dub-sar	scribe
dumu	son
^{d}dumu-zi	Dumuzi
dur-an-ki	Duranki
e-ne	he, she
e-ne—du$_{11}$	to play
e$_2$	house
e$_{11}$ (ed$_3$)	to ascend/descend
e$_2$-an-na	Eanna temple
e$_2$-gal	palace
e$_2$-ḫur-saĝ	Eḫursaĝ temple
e$_2$-kur	Ekur temple
e$_2$-maḫ	Emaḫ temple

e$_2$-ninnu	Eninnu temple
e$_3$	to go out
eden	steppe, plain
eme-gir$_{15}$	Emegir, native language
eme-ki-en-gi	Emekiengi, Sumerian
eme-sal	Emesal ("thin/fine tongue")
^{d}en-lil$_2$	Enlil
en$_3$—tar	to ask
ensi$_2$	ruler
^{giš}eren	cedar
eridu^{ki}	Eridu
eš$_3$	shrine
ga	milk
gaba	chest
gaba—ri	to confront
gaba-šu-ĝar	opponent, rival
gal	big, great
geme$_2$	female worker
gi$_4$	to turn, return
gid$_2$	to be long
gu$_3$—de$_2$	to speak
gu$_3$-de$_2$-a	Gudea
gu$_4$	ox
gu$_7$	to eat
gub	to stand

gul	to destroy
gu-za	chair
$^{d}\tilde{g}a_2$-tum$_3$-du$_{10}$	Ĝatumdu
$\tilde{g}al_2$	to be, exist; put
$\tilde{g}ar$	to set, place
$\tilde{g}en$	to go
$\tilde{g}eštin$	wine, vine
$\tilde{g}eštug_2$	ear, wisdom
$\tilde{g}i_6$-par$_4$	Gipar, cloister
$\tilde{g}iri_3$	road
$\tilde{g}ir_2$-su^{ki}	Girsu
$\tilde{g}iš$	wood
ḫal	to divide, distribute
ḫašḫur	apple
ḫul	to destroy, destruction
ḫul$_2$	to rejoice
ḫuluḫ	to be frightened
ḫur-sa$\tilde{g}$	mountain
i$_3$	oil
i$_7$ (id$_2$)	river
igi	eye
igi—bar	to look at
igi—$\tilde{g}ar$	to look at
il$_2$	to raise
im	clay

imin	seven
^dinanna	Inanna
inim	word
inim—gi$_4$	to reply, return a word
iti	month
ka	mouth
kal	rare, valuable
kala(g)	mighty
kalam	land
kar	quay
kar$_2$	to shine
kaš	beer
kaskal	road, journey
ki—ag̃$_2$	to love
ki—us$_2$	to set (firmly) on the ground; establish
ki-en-gi	Sumer
ki-uri	Akkad
ku$_3$	pure, holy
ku$_3$-babbar	silver
ku$_4$	to enter
kur	mountain, enemy land
la$_2$	to extend, hang
lamma	figurine deity
lil$_2$	wind, breeze
limmu$_2$	four

lipiš	inner body, heart, anger
lu$_2$	man, person
lugal	king
luḫ	to clean, wash
lul	untrue, false, criminal
ma$_2$	boat, ship
ma$_2$-gid$_2$	boat tower
maḫ	magnificent
mar-tu	westerner
maš$_2$	goat
maškim	administrator
me	divine power
me$_3$	battle, combat
me-a	where?
me-lim$_4$	frightening splendor
me-še$_3$	where to?
me-teš$_2$	praise
men	crown, tiara
mes	hero
mi$_2$	praise
mi$_2$—du$_{11}$	to care for, treat well
mir	to be angry
mu	name, text, year
mu$_2$	to grow
mu$_4$	to get dressed

mul	star, to shine
munus	woman
muš	snake
ᵍⁱˢna₂	bed
na₄	stone
nag̃	to drink
nam—ku₄	to curse
nam—tar	to decree a fate
nam-til₃	life
ᵈnanna	Nanna
nar	musician
ne₃	strength, force
nesag̃₂	first-fruit offering
ni₂ (I)	fear
ni₂ (II)	self
nibru^ki	Nippur
nig̃₂	thing
nig̃₂-du₇	appropriate thing
ᵈnimin-tab-ba	Nimintabba
nin	lady
ᵈnin-a-zu	Ninazu
ninda	bread
nindaba	(food) offering
ᵈnin-g̃ir₂-su	Ningirsu
ninnu	fifty

ᵈnin-sumun	Ninsumun
ᵈnin-sun	Ninsun
nita/nita₂	man, male
pa—e₃	to cause to appear
pad₃	to find
piriĝ	lion
ᵍⁱpisaĝ	reed basket
raḫ₂	to beat, kill
sag₃	to beat, strike
sag₉	to be good, beautiful
saĝ	head
saĝ—gid₂	to become angry
saĝ—il₂	to raise the head
saḫ₂	pig
sal	thin, fine
sar (I)	to write
sar (II)	to run, hasten
sed₄	to be cold
siskur₂	prayer, offering
su₁₃	to be long
ša₃	heart, middle
ša₃—ḫul₂	to be happy
še	grain
šir-bur-laᵏⁱ	Lagaš
šu	hand

šu—dab₅	to capture
šu—gid₂	to examine (extispicy)
šu—mu₂	to pray
šu—niĝin	to make a round trip
šu—tag	to decorate, touch
šu—zig₃	to raise the hand, to pray
šul-gi	Šulgi
šum₂	to give
tag	to touch
temen	foundation
til₃	to live
tir	forest
tud	to give birth
tug₂	clothing
tur	small, young
tuš	to sit
u₃	and
u₄	day
ur-ᵈnammu	Ur-Nammu
ur-saĝ	hero
uri₅ᵏⁱ	Ur
uru	city
zi	true
zig₃	to rise; raise

Appendix D

Glossary of Proper Nouns

Abzu	Freshwater ocean below the earth. Domain of the god Enki.
Akkad	City in Mesopotamia, capital of the Akkadian empire. Exact location unknown. Also used to refer to the northern region of lower Mesopotamia.
An	Sky god, also the Sumerian word for 'heaven'.
Anuna	General word for Mesopotamian gods. Associated with gods of the underworld in later periods.
Anzu	Mythological monster. Lion-headed eagle that could cause whirlwinds with its wings. Features prominently in mythology as both a benevolent and malevolant force.
Bagara	Temple of Ningirsu at Lagaš.
Bau	Goddess worshiped at Lagaš, spouse of Ningirsu. Daughter of

	An.
Bur-Suen	King of Isin. Ruled 1895-1874 B.C.E.
Der	City-state east of the Tigris, on the border between Sumer and Elam.
Dumuzi	Shepherd god, spouse/lover of Inanna.
Duranki	Temple, "Bond of Heaven and Earth". See: Ekur.
Eanna	Temple of Inanna at Uruk.
Eḫursaĝ	Temple built by Šulgi.
Ekur	Temple of Enlil at Nippur. Also known as "Duranki".
Emaḫ	Temple of Šara at Umma.
Eninnu	Temple of Ningirsu at Lagaš.
Enlil	One of the most important Mesopotamian gods, often called the 'king'. Features prominently in mythology.
Eridu	City, located in south-west Mesopotamia. Sacred to the god Enki.
Gudea	King of Lagaš. Ruled 2150-2125 B.C.E.

Gipar	Priestly residence, located in or near to the religious precint of a city.
Girsu	One of the earliest known cities of the world. Capital city and religious center of the Lagaš city-state.
Ĝatumdu	Goddess worshipped at Lagaš, later equated with Bau.
Inanna	Most important female deity in Mesopotamia. Goddess of love and warfare, syncretized to the goddess Ištar in later history. Closely connected with the city of Uruk. Spouse/lover of Dumuzi.
Lagaš	Sumerian city-state located by the Tigris river in southern Mesopotamia.
Nanna	Moon god, also: Suen, Sin. Closely connected with the city of Ur.
Nimintabba	Little known goddess, worshipped at a small temple at Ur.
Ninazu	Son of Ereškigal, goddess of the underworld. Connected with the

	underworld.
Ningirsu	Warrior god, chief god of Lagaš.
Ninsumun	See: Ninsun.
Ninsun	Goddess, wife of the divine king Lugalbanda and mother of Gilgameš.
Nippur	City in southern Mesopotamia, religious centre for much of Mesopotamian history.
Suen	Moon god, also: Nanna, Sin. Closely connected with the city of Ur.
Sumer	Southern Mesopotamia. When used in the title "king of Sumer and Akkad", used to denote control of the entirety of southern (lower) Mesopotamia.
Šulgi	Second king of the Third Dynasty of Ur. Ruled c. 2095-2047 B.C.E.
Ur	City in southern Mesopotamia on the bank of the Euphrates river, one of the world's first cities.
Ur-Nammu	First king of the Third Dynasty of Ur. Ruled c. 2112-2095 B.C.E.

Appendix E

Glossary of Common Irregular Verbs[61]

de$_6$ to bring

de$_6$ (*ḫ.* sg.); laḫ$_4$ (*ḫ.* pl.)

tum$_2$, tum$_3$ (*m.* sg.); laḫ$_4$ (*m.* pl.)

du$_{11}$ to say, speak

du$_{11}$ (*ḫ.* sg.); e (*ḫ.* pl.)

e (*m.* sg.); e (*m.* pl.)

e$_3$ to go out, bring out

e$_3$ (*ḫ.* sg., pl.)

e$_3$.d (*m.* sg., pl.)

gi$_4$ to turn, return

gi$_4$.gi$_4$ (*m.* sg., pl.)

gul   to destroy

gul.gul (*m.* sg., pl.)

g̃ar   to set, place

g̃a$_2$.g̃a$_2$ (*m.* sg., pl.)

g̃en   to go

g̃en (*ḫ.* sg.); (e).re$_7$ (*ḫ.* pl.)

---

[61] For a full catalogue of Sumerian verbal forms, Thomsen 1984 is the best resource. It is, unfortunately, incredibly difficult to find, so we have included some common irregular verbs here. Attinger's 2009 *Tableau grammatical du sumérien (problèmes choisis)* is also a useful resource, and is freely available online.

du (*m.* sg.); su$_8$.bi (*m.* pl.)

nag̃ to drink

na$_8$.na$_8$ (*m.* sg., pl.)

ra to beat

ra.ra (*m.* sg., pl.)

šag$_5$ to be/make good

ša$_6$.ša$_6$(.g) (*m.* sg., pl.)

te/ti to approach

te/ti (*ḫ.* sg. and pl.)

te.g̃/ti.g̃ (*m.* sg., pl.)

tuš to sit

tuš (*ḫ/m.* sg.); durun (*ḫ/m.* pl.)

uš$_2$ to die, kill

uš$_2$ (*ḫ.* sg.); ug$_5$, ug$_7$, ug$_7$.ug$_7$ (*ḫ.* pl.)

ug$_5$, ug$_7$ (*m.* sg., pl.)

zig$_3$ to rise, stand up

zi.zi (*m.* sg., pl.)

Appendix F

Cuneiform Sign List

This sign list contains all the cuneiform signs that appear in this book. Each sign is listed with the number assigned to it by a standard sign list used by Assyriology, "Altbabylonische Zeichenliste de sumerisch-literarischen Texte", by Catherine Mittermayer.

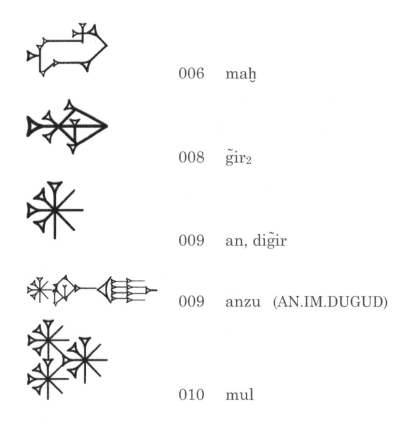

	006	maḫ
	008	g̃ir₂
	009	an, dig̃ir
	009	anzu (AN.IM.DUGUD)
	010	mul

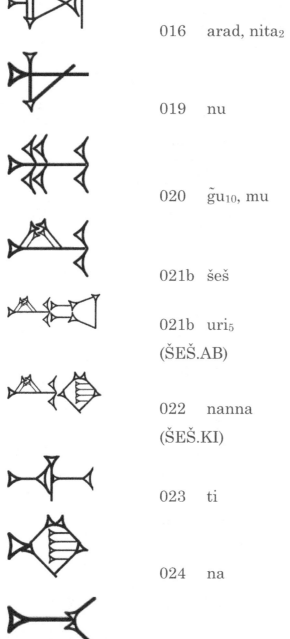

016   arad, nita$_2$

019   nu

020   g̃u$_{10}$, mu

021b   šeš

021b   uri$_5$
(ŠEŠ.AB)

022   nanna
(ŠEŠ.KI)

023   ti

024   na

025   bad

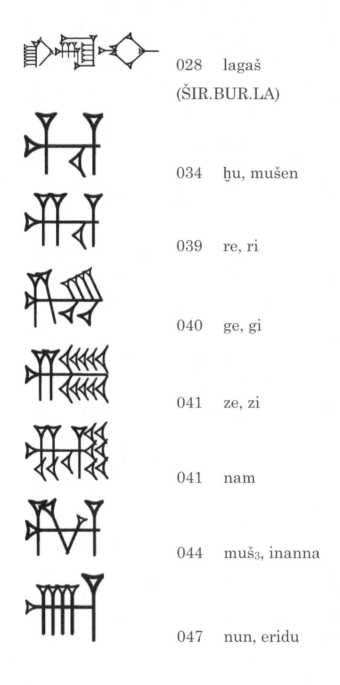

028　lagaš
(ŠIR.BUR.LA)

034　ḫu, mušen

039　re, ri

040　ge, gi

041　ze, zi

041　nam

044　muš₃, inanna

047　nun, eridu

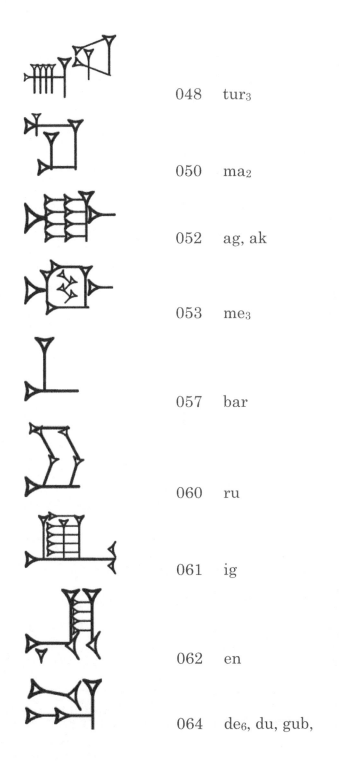

048   tur₃

050   ma₂

052   ag, ak

053   me₃

057   bar

060   ru

061   ig

062   en

064   de₆, du, gub,

		g̃en, tum$_2$
	067	dim$_2$, gin$_7$
	068	uš, us$_2$, nita
	094	ama
	107	e$_2$
	109	tab
	116	bi$_2$, de$_3$, ne
	118	gu$_4$
	120	ḫe$_2$
	123	ta

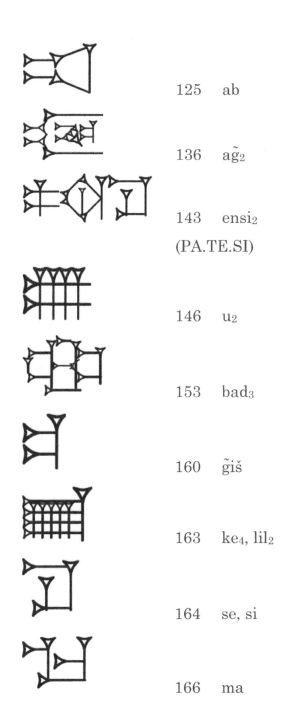

125 ab

136 ağ₂

143 ensi₂
(PA.TE.SI)

146 u₂

153 bad₃

160 ğiš

163 ke₄, lil₂

164 se, si

166 ma

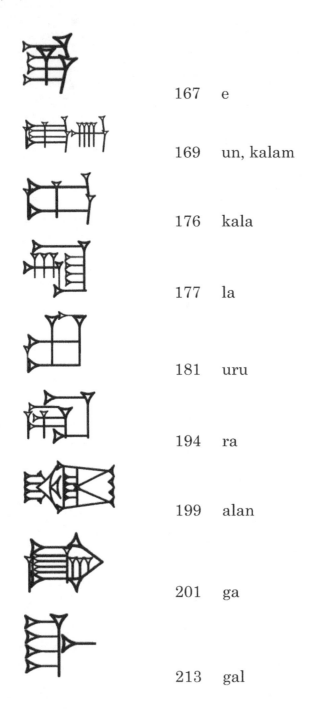

167 e

169 un, kalam

176 kala

177 la

181 uru

194 ra

199 alan

201 ga

213 gal

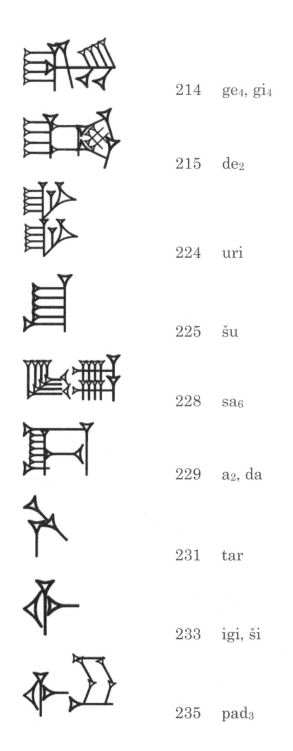

214 ge₄, gi₄

215 de₂

224 uri

225 šu

228 sa₆

229 a₂, da

231 tar

233 igi, ši

235 pad₃

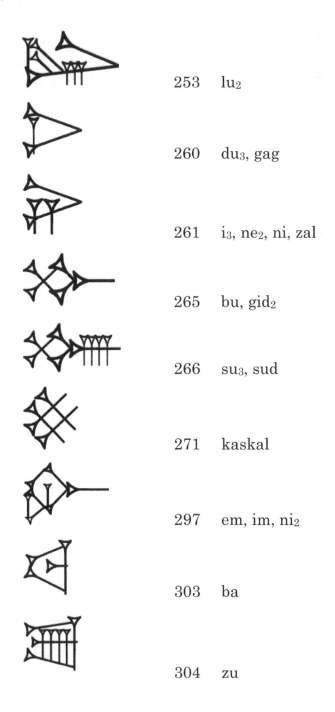

253	lu$_2$
260	du$_3$, gag
261	i$_3$, ne$_2$, ni, zal
265	bu, gid$_2$
266	su$_3$, sud
271	kaskal
297	em, im, ni$_2$
303	ba
304	zu

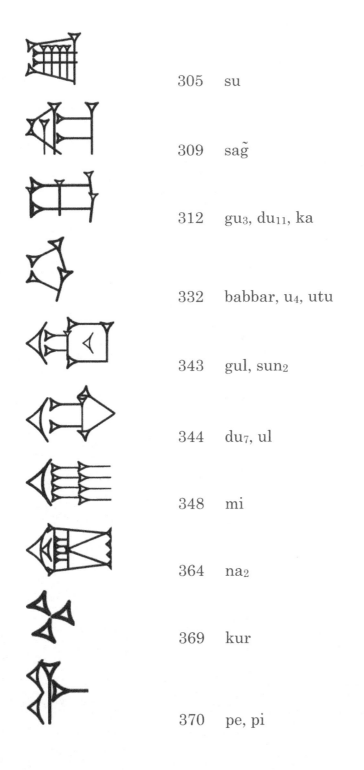

305   su

309   saĝ

312   gu$_3$, du$_{11}$, ka

332   babbar, u$_4$, utu

343   gul, sun$_2$

344   du$_7$, ul

348   mi

364   na$_2$

369   kur

370   pe, pi

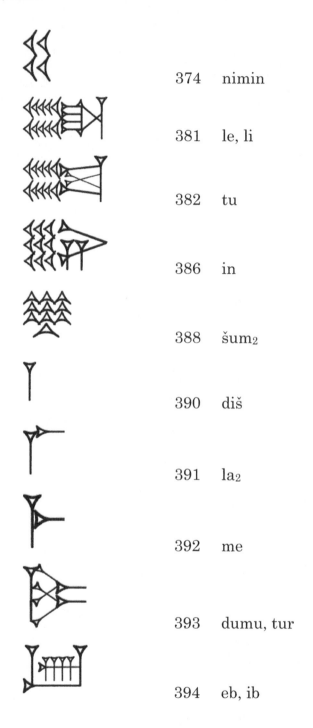

374	nimin
381	le, li
382	tu
386	in
388	šum₂
390	diš
391	la₂
392	me
393	dumu, tur
394	eb, ib

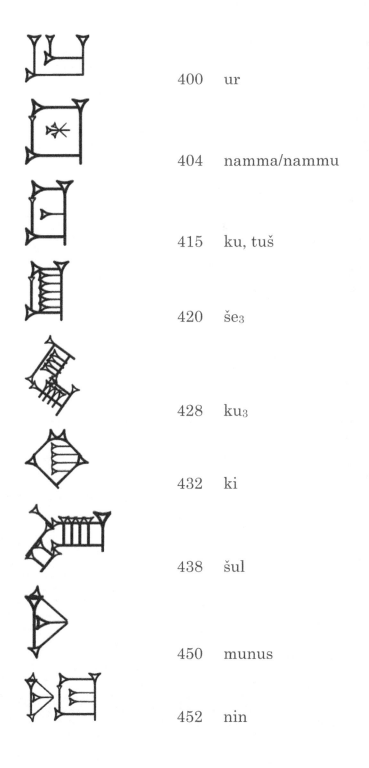

400 ur

404 namma/nammu

415 ku, tuš

420 še₃

428 ku₃

432 ki

438 šul

450 munus

452 nin

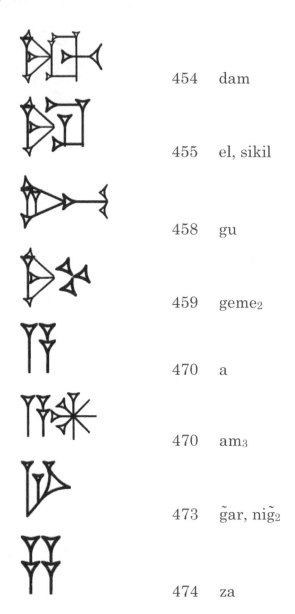

454	dam
455	el, sikil
458	gu
459	geme$_2$
470	a
470	am$_3$
473	g̃ar, nig̃$_2$
474	za

Appendix G

Glossary of Grammatical Terms

Ablative

Grammtical case, generally meaning "from" or "away from".

Active

When the subject of a verb acts or does something.

Agent

The subject of a transitive verb. See also: Subject.

Apposition

When two nouns or noun phrases, referring to the same thing, are placed next to each other in a sentence.

Animate

Humans or divine beings.

Anticipatory genitive

A method of indicating possession, formed by placing the genitival marker on the possessor, rather than the possessed object

Auslaut

The final consonant of a Sumerian word that is often carried over into subsequent grammatical features.

Auxiliary verb

/ak/ or /du$_{11}$/. Used in the verbal chain in place of a

compound verb when the compound verb is written elsewhere in the sentence.

Case element

Grammatical elements that indicate relationships between different parts of speech. See also: Case ending; Case marker.

Case ending

Grammatical element attached to a noun that indicates how the noun is functioning within the sentence.

Case marker

Grammatical elements found in the verbal chain that indicate the relationship between the verb and the rest of the sentence. See also: Case ending.

Cohortative

Modal prefix, meaning "let me/us".

Comitative

Grammatical case, generally meaning "with".

Compound noun

A noun formed by two or more cuneiform signs that have independent meanings.

Compound verb

A Sumerian verbal form made up of a noun and a governing verbal base.

Conjugation

The changes that occur in a verb to show tense, person,

and mood, etc.

Conjugation prefix

Prefix that usually appears at the beginning of the verbal chain. Certain prefixes often denote verbal nuances – i.e. active, passive, transitive, or intransitive.

Contraction

When some or all of a grammatical feature is omitted.

Copula

Forms of the verb 'to be', used as a standard ending attached to words or phrases.

Cuneiform

Writing system used in Mesopotamia from roughly 3200 B.C.E. until the 1st c. C.E.

Dative

Grammatical case, generally meaning 'to, for'.

Determinative

A sign indicating the category of a noun.

Direct object

The object that receives the action of a verb.

Equative

Grammatical case, generally meaning "like, as".

Ergative

Grammatical case that marks the agent (subject of a transitive verb) of a sentence, usually marked with an /-e/.

First person

Agent or subject of a verb "I/we".

Genitive

Marker of possession.

Ḫamtu

Sumerian "past tense".

Homophonous

Two or more words that are spelled differently, but pronounced the same.

Imperative

Verbal construction used to give an order.

Inanimate

Animals and objects.

Independent pronoun

Personal pronoun unattached to a verb – i.e. "you", "they", "he/she"

Inflection

The ways in which a word can change in order to alter its meaning. See also: Conjugation

Intransitive

A verb without a direct object

Lexical form

Form of a word found in a dictionary.

Locative

Grammatical case, generally indicating proximity in(to)/within a physical location.

Locative-terminative

Grammatical case, generally indicating motion towards a location.

Logogram

A sign representing a whole word or concept.

Marû

Sumerian "present/future tense".

Modal prefix

Prefix at the beginning of a verbal chain that changes the nuance of the verb with respect to things like permission, desire, ability, etc.

Negation

Modal prefix /nu-/ which changes a verb into a negative.

Non-finite form

Verbal forms that are not conjugated verbs (infinitives, participles, etc.).

Normalize

Writing the grammatical structure represented by a set of Sumerian signs.

Number

Whether a verb is singular ("I", "he/she") or plural ("we/they").

Object

Part of speech in a sentence that receives the effect of a verb, directly or indirectly.

Oblique object

The direct object of a compound verb, marked gramatically with the locative-terminative, locative, or no marking.

Paradigm

A chart or list showing all of the ways a verb, noun, etc. can be written to account for things like person, number, tense, etc.

Participle

Words that look like verbs, but are used like adjectives or nouns.

Passive

When the subject receives the action of a transitive verb.

Personal pronoun

A pronoun that refers to a particular (grammatical) person (I, you, they).

Phonetic

Representing the sound of language.

Possessive pronoun

Pronouns which indicate possession (i.e. his, hers).

Precative

A modal prefix that is generally translated "let him/her".

Prefix

Grammatical element written before (and, in Sumerian, sometimes after!) the verbal base of a verbal chain

Preposition

Word describing the relationship between a noun or pronoun and another word in a sentence.

Purpose clause

A clause best translated as "in order to...".

Reduplication

Repeating a word, usually to indicate plurality.

Regular verb

A verbal base that does not change its form depending on the tense or person.

Second person

"You".

Subject

The actor of a verb (in Sumerian, we use this to describe the "actor" in an intransitive verb). See also: Agent.

Suffix

A group of letters added to the end of a word to modify its meaning.

Syllable

Single unit of a spoken language.

Tense

Whether a verb is indicating that the action has or will happen in the past, present, or future.

Terminative

Grammatical case, generally meaning "to, toward".

Third person

"He/she/it", "they".

Transitive

A verb with a direct object.

Verbal base

The part of the verbal chain that carries the primary meaning of the verb.

Verbal chain

The Sumerian verb, along with any prefixes or suffixes that modify its meaning.

Word order

The manner or order in which a sentence is constructed.

Appendix H

Index to Cuneiform Sources

Inscription 1	RIME 3/1.1.7.1
Inscription 2	RIME 3/1.1.7.10
Inscription 3	RIME 3/1.1.7.20
Inscription 4	RIME 3/1.1.7.21
Inscription 5	RIME 3/1.1.7.30
Inscription 6	RIME 3/1.1.7.40
Inscription 7	RIME 3/1.1.7.50
Inscription 8	RIME 3/2.1.1.23
Inscription 9	RIME 3/2.1.1.24
Inscription 10	RIME 3/2.1.1.25
Inscription 11	RIME 4.1.7.2
Inscription 12	RIME 4.1.7.2002
Year Name 1	Šulgi 1
Year Name 2	Šulgi 6
Year Name 3	Šulgi 10
Year Name 4	Šulgi 16
Year Name 5	Šulgi 21
Year Name 6	Šulgi 22
Year Name 7	Šulgi 37
Hand Copy 1	P226644
Hand Copy 2	P226818
Hand Copy 3	P232332
Hand Copy 4	P226202

Bibliography

Attinger, Pascal

    1993 *Eléments de linguistique sumérienne: la construction de du11/e/di 'dire'*. Germany: Vanderhoeck & Ruprecht.

    2009 *Tableau grammatical du sumérien (problèmes choisis)*. Bern.

Black, Jeremy and Green, Anthony.

    2004 *Gods, Demons, and Symbols of Ancient Mesopotamia. An Illustrated Dictionary*. London: The British Museum Press.

Edzard, Dietz-Otto.

    1997 *Gudea and His Dynasty*. Royal Inscriptions of Mesopotamia 3/1. Toronto: University of Toronto Press.

    2003 *Sumerian Grammar*. Handbook of Oriental Studies. Boston, MA: Brill.

Frayne, Douglas.

1990 *Old Babylonian Period (2003-1595 BC)*. Royal Inscriptions of Mesopotamia 4. Toronto: Toronto University Press.

1997 *Ur III Period (2112-2004 BC)*. Royal Inscriptions of Mesopotamia 3/2. Toronto: Toronto University Press.

Foxvog, Daniel.

2016 *Introduction to Sumerian Grammar*. CreateSpace Independent Publishing Platform.

Hayes, John.

2018 *A Manual of Sumerian Grammar and Texts, Third Revised and Expanded Edition*. Malibu, CA: Undena Publications.

Jagersma, Abraham H.

2010 *A Descriptive Grammar of Sumerian*. Dissertation. Netherlands: Leiden University.

Sigirst, Marcel and Gomi, Tohru.

1991 *The Comprehensive Catalogue of
Published Ur III Tablets.* Bethesda,
MD: CDL Press.

Thomsen, Marie-Louise.

1984 *The Sumerian Language: an
Introduction to its History and
Grammatical Structure.*
Mesopotamia 10. Copenhagen:
Akademisk Forlag.

Zólyomi, Gábor.

2017 *An Introduction to the Grammar of
Sumerian.* Budapest: Eötvös
University Press

Made in United States
Orlando, FL
25 September 2023